THE GOD ARGUMENT

A. C. GRAYLING is Professor of Philosophy at and Master of the New College of the Humanities, London. He believes that philosophy should take an active, useful role in society and is a prolific author, whose books include philosophy, ethics, biography, history, drama and essays. He has been a regular contributor to *The Times, Financial Times, Observer, Independent on Sunday, Economist, Literary Review, New Statesman* and Prospect, and is a frequent and popular contributor to radio and television programmes, including *Newsnight, Today, In Our Time, Start the Week* and *CNN News*. Among his recent books are *Towards the Light: The Story of the Struggle for Liberty and Rights that Made the Modern West, Liberty in the Age of Terror* and *The Good Book: A Secular Bible*.

OTHER BOOKS BY A. C. GRAYLING

THE GOD ARGUMENT

The Case *against* Religion
and *for* Humanism

A. C. Grayling

BLOOMSBURY

LONDON · NEW DELHI · NEW YORK · SYDNEY

First published in Great Britain 2013
This paperback edition published 2014

Bloomsbury Publishing Plc
50 Bedford Square
London WC1B 3DP

www.bloomsbury.com

Bloomsbury Publishing, London, New Delhi, New York and Sydney

A CIP catalogue record for this book is available from the British Library

ISBN 978 1 4088 3743 6

10 9 8 7 6 5 4 3 2 1

Typeset by Hewer Text UK Ltd, Edinburgh
Printed in Great Britain by CPI Group (UK) Ltd, Croydon CR0 4YY

Esse aliquid invictum, esse aliquem in quem nihil fortuna possit,
e re publica est generis humani.

SENECA, *De Constantia*, XIX.4

Contents

PART II: *For* Humanism

Acknowledgements

We learn from example as much as from study. My thanks go to colleagues and fellows in the cause: Andrew Copson, Richard Dawkins, Daniel Dennett, Derren Brown, Steven Pinker, Robin Ince, Sam Harris, Keith PorteousWood, Terry Sanderson, Roy Brown, Leo Igwe, Peter Cave and many others whose views and contributions have variously provided instruction or enjoyment or both. During the writing of this book the world lost two eloquent and forceful comrades in the task, Paul Kurtz and Christopher Hitchens. The latter's lost is personally felt.

Every generation thinks it travels an especially difficult road, and in one good sense that is true: for every generation must travel its own road, but with the hope of arriving at a destination further along than its predecessors. The hope in this case is that our contributions will each add their inches to that forward motion, and that one day there will be arrival. With so many people like those named making their contributions, perhaps that day is no longer distant.

The final draft of what follows was revised in the beauty and tranquillity of Le Radicchie near San Donato under the

Tuscan sun, courtesy of Melanie and Piers Gibson, whose hospitable good company is very warmly acknowledged.

As always, thanks beyond words go to Katie Hickman, *sine quo non*.

Introduction

Religious faith has many manifestations. There are people of sincere piety for whom the religious life is a source of deep and powerful meaning. For them and for others, a spiritual response to the beauty of the world, the vastness of the universe, and the love that can bind one human heart to another, feels as natural and necessary as breathing. Some of the art and music that has been inspired by faith counts among the loveliest and most moving expressions of human creativity. It is indeed impossible to understand either history or art without an understanding of what people believed, feared and hoped through their religious conceptions of the world and human destiny. Religion is a pervasive fact of history, and has to be addressed as such.

In others of its manifestations, religious faith is neither so kind nor so attractive. History attests to the weight of suffering that religious tyranny and conflict have together generated, from individuals struggling with feelings of sinfulness because of perfectly natural desires, to nations and civilisations engulfed in war and atrocity by interreligious hatreds. Religions have often been cruel in their effects, and remain so today: homosexuals are hanged in Iran, adulterous women are beheaded in Afghanistan and stoned to death in Saudi Arabia, 'witches' are murdered in Africa, women and children are subordinated in fundamentalist households in the Bible Belt of the United States and in many parts of the Islamic world. Throughout history the religion-inspired suppression of women has robbed humanity of at least half its potential creativity and genius.

Whereas the consolations of religion are mainly personal, the burdens are social and political as well as personal. This is one argument for greater secularism, a main form of which asks religion to keep itself in the private sphere, and not to obtrude into matters of general public concern. Committed followers of religion oppose this, on the grounds that because they possess the truth about things, and in particular about what their deity wants everyone in the world to think and do, they have a duty to lead everyone in that direction. For the zealous among them this is a matter of urgency, for in their chosen direction – so they believe – lies salvation, truth and eternal life. Those who disagree with them see this as just one more attempt by one group to impose its views and its authority on everyone else. As history shows, the competition that arises between different religious outlooks when any one of them tries to dominate, readily leads to trouble.

But the case against religion goes deeper than an argument for secularism. It is that religion's claims and beliefs do not stand up to examination. Briefly put, critical examination of religion's claims places it in the same class as astrology and magic. Like these systems of thought, religion dates from mankind's less educated and knowledgeable early history, and like them it has been superseded by advances in our understanding of the world and ourselves. Or should have been superseded: its survival, as with the survival of astrology and other outlooks from the past, is the prompt for critical discussion of its claims and outlook.

With regard to the good things attributed to religion – the consolation and inspiration it provides, which it provides even if it is false – the critics of religion have a view. It is that there are other and better sources of these valuable things, which have the additional merit of being far better grounded in reason and a more accurate understanding of the world – which is in short to say: are far closer to the truth.

In respect of the atrocities and oppressions too frequently caused by religion, its defenders say that this is the work of sinful man, not the religion itself. Religion's critics reply that whether the atrocities and oppressions are the work of man or the work of the religion, either way these are the very reasons why it is time to go beyond religion, and to invite people to a truer and healthier view both of the world and of the source of what is good in human life.

And indeed, everywhere that science and education have advanced, so religion has dwindled in influence. Where it retains a hold on the personal lives of people in more advanced and educated societies, it almost always does so in a much modified form to make it more consistent with modern life. Increased liberty of thought and expression has allowed those who do not hold religious views to express their criticism openly, and religion's traditional armour of privilege and respect has accordingly rusted away, increasingly exposing it to challenge.

Religious individuals and institutions feel under pressure because of this, and sometimes accuse their critics of militancy. The critics reply that when religion occupied a dominant position in society, it dealt with its critics much more harshly than today's critics now deal with religion: for one familiar example, by torturing them and burning them at the stake. Today's critics of religion generally restrict themselves to hurling arguments rather than stones at the religious.

Although history is moving in the right direction from the point of view of those who wish to see the human mind liberated from religion and superstition, and although this impetus has been powerfully aided by the work of Richard Dawkins, Victor Stenger, Daniel Dennett, Sam Harris, Dan Barker, the late and much lamented Christopher Hitchens and others, there are two major tasks outstanding.

One is to deal with what religious apologists say in defending themselves from the arguments of those just listed.

The other is to show that there is a beautiful and life-enhancing alternative outlook that offers insight, consolation, inspiration and meaning, which has nothing to do with religion, and everything to do with the best, most generous, most sympathetic understanding of human reality.

The first task remains because, to put the matter graphically, contesting religion is like engaging in a boxing match with jelly: it is a shifting, unclear, amorphous target, which every blow displaces to a new shape. This is in large part because the religious themselves often do not have clear ideas, or much agreement among themselves, about what is meant by 'religion', 'god', 'faith' and associated concepts. And this is not surprising given the fact that these concepts are so elastic, multiple and ill-defined as to make it hard to attach a literal meaning to them.

But it is also because the justifications offered by religious people for their beliefs very often turn out to be post facto rationalisations for something that in its deepest depths is non-rational – something emotional, traditional, its roots almost always in the experiences of childhood when trusted adults instilled a religion-involving, and often an explicitly religious, way of viewing the world.

The combination of these facts explains why religion is such an amorphous target. Anyone who has studied a little logic knows that any claim, proposition or belief whatever is consistent with a contradiction or a meaningless statement. Religious ideas and commitments are, on examination, so characterised by ambiguity, multiplicity, a Babel of interpretations and significations, and indeed plain contradiction, that they are easily rendered consistent with any attempt to counter them.

Thus cancer, disability, tsunamis that kill tens of thousands including babies and old folk – all are, in the eyes of the faithful, regarded as consistent with the existence of a benevolent and omnipotent god. After an earthquake that kills many and destroys what had been built by the careful and long-term efforts of both the victims and the survivors, people go to church to give thanks and to pray for the dead – with no sense of irony or inconsistency. For what do they give thanks? That their gods, or the world designed by their gods, arbitrarily or otherwise destroyed and killed? Perhaps they give thanks that they were not among the crushed. Might not prayer that succeeded in averting the suffering, or in averting the earthquake, be regarded as more to the point?

Such thoughts are either dismissed, or answered by acceptance of the claim that some greater purpose has been served. Yet note that if a terrorist had killed that many or destroyed that much, his act would be regarded as an extreme atrocity by an evil agent.

Religious apologists are able to regard the imperfection and harshness of the world, and the presence in it of natural

and moral evil, as consistent with the existence of an interested deity, by saying that the deity's intentions are a mystery,
or that we are being tested, or that it is our fault for sinfully
employing the free will we have been given. Since very few
human parents would inflict on their children what a
supposed deity inflicts on the conscious parts of its creation,
this sounds like a particularly fine example of special
pleading.

These considerations only scratch the surface of the problem. That religion has survived so long is remarkable evidence
of how effectively it inculcates a mindset in which criticism
or questioning, and the recognition of contradiction or unac-
ceptability, is suppressed. This is not a careless claim. Only
consider: all forms of fundamentalism are notable for the
infantilising and blinding effect they have on their votaries.
Think of the angry crowds of Muslims demonstrating over
cartoons they find insulting. Murder is committed because
of this, and mayhem along with it. Mass immaturity of this
kind requires a pervasive culture of unthinking credulity to
foster it.

But one should not only look at fundamentalists, or fundamentalist types of religion. Non-fundamentalist religion, by
definition, depends upon cherry-picking the given religion's
doctrines, discarding the uncongenial teachings and reinter-
preting the others to make them more comfortable to live
with. Think, for example, of the fact that the majority of
Roman Catholics use contraception. The word that accurately and simply describes cherry-picking – choosing
manageable commitments and ignoring inconvenient ones
– is not a comfortable word; it is 'hypocrisy'. But it is done
with a blitheness, and often with a lack of self-awareness, that
religion in some of its forms deliberately seems to promote,

preferring half a loaf of adherence to no bread. But the concern for religion's critics is that where there are moderates, not far behind there will always be zealots.

For these reasons it is necessary to continue the debate until the unclarities and, too often, the evasions and rationalisations of religion have been fully examined, and the last resort – 'I just choose to believe, despite everything' – has itself been investigated and challenged.

That is the task of the first part of this book: to set out the case against religion – religion as such, in any form. Because of the shifting and often deliberately obscure nature of religious ideas, I do this by, so to speak, following the ball wherever it rolls, interweaving the considerations that have to be raised as they occur – historical, psychological, scientific, philosophical. It is a game of shadows, made no easier by the fact that many of the apologists and votaries of religion are eager to believe, even to self-deceive, and refuse to examine the considerations that would call their cherished commitments into question. There is a human tragedy in this: the more they suspect that they might be wrong, the more fiercely they adhere. Mark Twain put the point accurately if a little unkindly: 'faith is believing what you know ain't so'.

In my view, the argument against religion is an argument for the liberation of the human mind, and the possibility of at last formulating an ethical outlook that all humankind can share, thus providing a basis for a much more integrated and peaceful world.

This is a theme that is much more interesting to me personally, and is the substance of the second part of the book: an account of the better alternative to religion, the humane and positive outlook of an ethics free from religious or superstitious aspects, an outlook that has its roots in rich philosophical traditions, yet is far more attuned to our contemporary world, and far more sensitive to the realities of human experience, than religion is.

This is an outlook that the general term 'humanism' now denotes. It is an outlook of great beauty and depth, premised on kindness and common sense, drawing its principles from a conversation about the good whose roots lie in the philosophical debates of classical antiquity, continually enriched by the insights and experience of thinkers, poets, historians and scientists ever since. To move from the Babel of religions and their claims, and from the too often appalling effects of religious belief and practice on humankind, to the life-enhancing insights of the humanist tradition which most of the world's educated and creative minds have embraced, is like escaping from a furnace to cool waters and green groves. I hope the latter is the destination of all humanity, as more people come to understand this ethical outlook as far the better alternative.

Humanism, accordingly, is the answer to the question often asked amidst the acerbic debates between proponents and opponents of religion: what alternative can the non-religious offer to religion as the focus for expression of those spiritual yearnings, that nostalgia for the absolute, the profound bass-note of emotion that underlies the best and deepest parts of ourselves? Often this question is asked rhetorically, as if there is no answer to it, the assumption being that by default religion is the only thing that speaks to these aspects of human experience, even if religion is false and merely symbolic. The symbolism, some views have it, is enough to do the work.

Humanism is the emphatic answer to the request for an alternative. As I aim to show in the second half of this book, the most wonderful resources for good and flourishing lives lie in the intelligence, the experience, the wisdom and insight of our fellows in the human story; and it is from these resources that the humanist outlook derives.

PART I

Against Religion

I

Clarifications

To put matters at their simplest, the major reason for the continuance of religious belief in a world which might otherwise have long moved beyond it, is indoctrination of children before they reach the age of reason, together with all or some combination of social pressure to conform, social reinforcement of religious institutions and traditions, emotion, and (it has to be said) ignorance – of science, of psychology, of history in general, and of the history and actual doctrines of religions themselves.

This statement doubtless sounds polemical, but that is not the intention; rather, it is a setting out of considered facts, each discussed later in these pages. They are important facts, because understanding them is essential to solving one of the world's greatest problems: how to free the mind of humankind from attitudes and practices which are among the biggest impediments to peace and human progress, and to adopt in their place the humane outlook that is seriously concerned to promote both, and has a real chance of doing it.

In the Introduction it was acknowledged that religious belief can serve as a comfort, guide and inspiration when

benign, while stating the less comfortable and larger truth
that religion is far too often a form of enslavement, mental
and even literal, and a source of harm from which the world
needs liberation. Whereas there are other sources of individual comfort and inspiration that are far better than
religion – they include love and friendship, family life, art,
the pursuit of knowledge and, as noted, the outlook and
principles of humanism – there are very few sources of
conflict and mental enslavement as bad as an ideology which
demands self-abnegation by submission to its dogmas and to
the self-appointed interpreters of its dogmas. Religion is the
paradigm of this.

So the argument cannot be that the world needs to rid
itself of 'bad religion' in order to promote 'good religion'
in its stead, for alas history and contemporary affairs overwhelmingly teach a different lesson. What tries to be
'good' or moderate religion is invariably a faint version of
its official self, existing only when its votaries have rejected
most of the doctrines and practices associated with it. To
make a moderate version of their religion they cherry-
pick the bits they can live with: the moment anything
more serious in the way of commitment and belief enters
the frame, threats immediately arise to women, gays,
human rights, peace itself – and this whether you are in
the Christian southern states of the United States, Jewish
ultra-Orthodox settlements in the Palestinian territories,
or Muslim-majority countries or communities anywhere
in the world. 'True' versions of these religions are by their
nature fundamentalist, while 'moderate' versions of religions are temporisations; the path from the latter to the
former is short for anyone on whom the enthusiasms of
faith take a grip.

Accordingly, when we engage with the reasons for the survival of what is essentially a stone-age outlook in the modern world, it is difficult not to sound polemical; but this is chiefly because the first step in properly discussing religion requires plain speaking – and plain speaking naturally enough sounds harsh when it is about something that for very many centuries has protected itself from scrutiny and challenge by demanding uncritical deference and respect, and too often by hiding behind a smokescreen of what are claimed to be sacred mysteries.

The sophisticated apparatuses of worldwide religious organisations, the polysyllabic treatises of theologians, and the huge congregations of megachurches chanting ecstatically and holding their hands aloft, give the impression that there must be something more significant at the basis of religion's continuance in the world – indeed, a god, or more accurately an entire other reality, a non-material universe according to some views filled with divine beings, saints, angels and demons.

For religious apologists, assuming or asserting the existence of a supernatural agency in the universe, and moreover one that is interested in human beings on this planet, is the basis they claim for the phenomenon of religion. On this view religion is a response to a transcendent fact, the existence of that other supposed reality containing at least one supernatural being.

The alternative view, the view of religion's critics, is that religions are man-made affairs, their roots in early human experience, with all the consequences of this for the metaphysics and morality constituting them. On this view it is no surprise that religion is at odds with so much of what has happened in history and the world today. From this tension comes much harm, to individuals and societies both. Given that the case against religion is an overwhelming one, freeing the world from its influence has to be an urgent goal, however difficult it might seem to achieve.

The first step is to introduce some clarity into the concepts we are dealing with, and to put them into perspective.

Given that the word 'religion' is used to denote such a wide range of phenomena, we have to identify firm central examples. Obvious and unequivocal candidates are Judaism, Christianity, Islam and the various aspects of what British colonial authorities in nineteenth-century India chose to call 'Hinduism'.

We have to be similarly firm in distinguishing between outlooks and practices that are properly called 'religions' and those that are in fact not religions but philosophies. This is a very important distinction, and one that is widely over-looked. Thus, Buddhism in its original form, and still in the Theravada (Small Vehicle) form, is a philosophy, not a religion. So is Jainism, so most emphatically is Confucianism. The differentiator is that these philosophies are not centred upon belief in, worship of, and obedience to a deity or deities, from whom or from which come the commands that construct the correct form of life and belief for the devotee.

Buddhism and Jainism involve metaphysical views that prompt some to assimilate them to religion, but this is a bad mistake. It is a similar mistake to the one that makes many people think that typical faith religions such as Christianity and Islam are the same kind of thing as the public cohesion practices of, say, Roman religion, or (an even worse mistake!) the philosophy of Stoicism. In this latter case, Stoic references to a principle of reason and order in the universe (the *logos*) are interpreted as amounting to a religious commitment of some sort. But what the Stoics meant by *logos* is a universal principle of reason, identified with the order of nature. It is not a god; Stoics did not pray to it or worship it. Jainism likewise has no god. The *tian* of Confucianism is in effect the same as the *logos* of the Stoics, and is not even remotely a god, goddess or divine entity, still less a transcendent one.

Another important distinction is that between superstition and religion. All religious people are superstitious, but not all superstitious people are religious. To generalise mightily but not inaccurately, the Chinese are not a religious people, but they are very superstitious (this accepts that a minor percentage of the Chinese population are religious; some are Christian – the work of missionaries – or members of Falun Gong and the like: but the operative phrase here is 'minor percentage' of a vast population). This fact about the Chinese, the most numerous people on Earth and a large fraction of the Earth's human population, gives the lie to the theory that belief in a god is hard-wired in the human brain.

An important rider to the distinction between religions and philosophies is that all religions properly so called, and some philosophies, including most political philosophies, are members of a single category, the category of *ideology*. Noticing this has powerful explanatory value. The Christianity of Torquemada's Inquisition and Stalinism in the Soviet Union were both ideologies that asserted that there is one great truth, and therefore one correct way to live and behave; and that therefore everyone must sign up for it, and any deviation from it was heresy (or 'counter-revolution'), punishable even by death.

One of many reasons for pointing this out is that freedom from coercive ideology is both a human right and a fundamental civil liberty, which is why *freedom from* religion should figure in any codification of human rights alongside the freedom to have a religion. The right to freedom from religion also means freedom from proselytisation or coercive demands to belong to one, or harassment and punishment for not belonging to one, and – very importantly – from the requirement to live according to the tenets or demands of a religion to which one does not subscribe. As it happens, this right is entailed by the right to self-determination, a fact which is insufficiently recognised and acted upon. The juxtaposition of a right to a religion and a right to freedom from religion entails that freedom to have a religion is not the same thing as the freedom to impose it on anyone else. The only major religion that does not habitually attempt to impose itself on others is Judaism, except that of course, like all the others, it indoctrinates very young, intellectually defenceless children, which is mainly how religions survive.

As implied by the foregoing, to attach a workable general definition to the word 'religion' is both necessary in discussions of this kind, and not easy given the indeterminacy of religious apologists' own many understandings of the term.

One way of dealing with the problem is to tackle it by looking at the contrast between what in general non-religious people say about what they believe and why they believe it, as against the kinds of things that religious people say they believe and why they believe them, as follows.

Everyone possesses many non-religious beliefs, but what distinguishes these from religious beliefs is the grounds on which they are held, and what they are about. Someone who does not hold religious beliefs would be likely to say that he or she holds a naturalistic world-view, that is, a view to the

effect that what exists is the realm of n
natural laws. This is accordingly a world-vi
observation, reason and science, and excludes
faith-involving element, and specifically excludes ben
invocation of a being or beings of a transcendent, supernatural, divine or mystical nature. By 'faith' is meant belief
held independently of whether there is testable evidence in
its favour, or indeed even in the face of counter-evidence.
This latter is regarded as a virtue in most religions; in
Christianity the case of Doubting Thomas is held out as
illustrating the point.

What centrally constitutes the standard examples of religions – Judaism, Christianity, Islam – is faith in the existence
of a supernatural, transcendent, divine being (or beings, if
one includes angels, saints, demons or other personae of the
given deity), and they further involve espousal of values and
practices taken to be required in response to the existence of
these beings, including worship and praise of it or them,
submission and obedience to the commands taken to emanate
from it or them, and so on.

Judaism, Christianity and Islam identify historical human
figures who enjoyed a special relationship with the beings in
question – prophets, Jesus, Mohammed – and who were
therefore able to transmit their teachings, requirements,
admonishments, promises, warnings, threats, and more, to
whomever would listen.

This follows a pattern found in earlier and other religions
– Zoroastrianism, for example. Jesus is alone among the
Judaic prophets in attaining divine status, or rather in being
actually identified with the deity for whom he began as a
spokesperson; but even in terms of religion in general he is
not unique, for in the mythologies pre-dating Christianity

...any heroic figures underwent apotheosis and joined their fathers or fellow gods in heaven or on Olympus.

In this focal sense, a religion not only involves a belief in the existence of a god or gods and perhaps other beings, that is, non-natural beings either in or (if transcendent) outside, yet connected to, the universe, but also that the relation of these beings to the universe is significant – centrally, by at least one of them being some or all of the universe's creator, ruler and moral law-giver.

The *meaning* of most of these remarks is, of necessity, merely notional. People think they understand what is being asserted, but on inspection a considerable degree of vagueness enters. It is hard to make literal sense of much theological and religious discourse, which is the reason that religious apologists, when pressed, resort to claims of ineffability concerning the central religious subject-matters and the inability of human minds to grasp them. Divine reality is, they say, too complex, mysterious and vast for comprehension. Apologists are here implicitly trading on the distinction between a capacity to *imagine* or *fantasise* something and the capacity to *conceive* of it – that is, form a coherent concept of it. One can believe that one in some sense understands the idea of a being or entity existing outside space and time, while yet possessed of miraculous or magical powers that enable it to intervene within space and time, and so forth – but to form a concept of such a thing is quite another matter.

A good illustration of the capacity to imagine or fantasise what cannot properly be conceived is given by science fiction, cartoon films and special effects in cinema productions. It can also be understood by noting that language is infinite (you can generate an infinitely long sentence by repeatedly using connectives such as 'and' and 'but') whereas

our intelligence is finite, which means that we cannot understand every grammatically well-formed sentence that can be
generated by language's recursive rules. Indeed, since we can
utter sentences that express logical impossibilities, it is easy to
show this. Consider the sentence, 'I can trisect a Euclidean
angle using only ruler and compass.' This is a grammatical
and even in one sense intelligible sentence, but it claims
something that is logically impossible to do – and therefore
to think. So we can say things (and imagine that we *sort of*
understand them) that do not express coherent thoughts.

Despite the fact that religious and theological sentences
very often say only apparently meaningful things, the formulation given above – that religion consists focally in belief in
non-natural agency or agencies with significant interests in
human activity on this planet, or whose existence makes
some necessary material difference to human beings –
roughly indicates what religious apologists take themselves to
believe. (Some people might believe that there are such entities but that they are not interested in human experience or
have no relationship to the immanent universe: functionally
this is a view that does no work and can be left aside.) It is a
separate matter that what is believed remains unclear; the
apologist will attribute this to the ineffability of things divine.

In sum and in brief, then, a religion is a set of beliefs and
practices focused on a god or gods. This is what I shall understand by 'religion' in all that follows.

2

Naming and Describing a 'god'

The next problem is the word 'god' itself, and the word with a capitalised 'g', 'God', to make it appear to function as a name.

Religious people of course use the word as a name or proper noun. Such uses, even by non-religious people, appear to imply or assume the existence of an entity thus named or referred to. The shorthand convenience of this usage perpetuates the illusion that there is a genuine subject of discussion in hand, and prevents people from distinguishing between the existence of religions – whose existence is a sociological fact – and the existence of gods, goddesses and other supernatural entities which those religions assert to exist – whose existence is a creation of man's imagination. If we used the phrases 'gods and goddesses' or 'supernatural agencies' when discussing what religious people believe exists, we would have a clearer view of the task that the debate addresses.

Because history's many religions are a sociological fact they are certainly worth discussing, but the many versions of supernatural entities that figure in those religions are only discussable as components of them. Yet there is a

near-universal assumption that 'god' is a word that refers to
something other than an idea, that its referent is something
one can 'believe in' and variously obey, fear, worship, praise,
have a relationship with, and invoke to explain a wide variety
of things, such as the origin of the universe, the intricacies of
nature, the foundation of moral principles, the purpose of
life, and more.

Even more significantly for religious people, the word is
typically invoked to denote the all-encompassing and unan-
swerable source of authority governing what people can
think, say, eat and wear, in what circumstances and with
whom they can have sexual relations, how they must behave
on specified days or weeks of the year, and so comprehen-
sively on. The fact that different religions claim that their
god or gods have different requirements in these respects
should be evidence that religions are man-made and historically conditioned, but religious people think that this insight
only applies to other people's religions, not their own.

What these considerations show is that if these sorts of
claims are to have content, we need to know what it is that
is putatively denoted by 'god' or 'God', so that we can judge
whether such a thing or things exist and have what it takes to
give them this significance.

And this, of course, proves very difficult. It is interesting to
try a minor thought experiment regarding the use of the word
'God' as a name or description. In such sentences as 'God
created the universe' or 'God forbids homosexual acts', remove
the word 'God' and substitute the name 'Fred' or the description 'the supreme egg'. That name and that description are
arbitrarily chosen to fill the space in sentences that 'God' occu-
pies, in order to test how much explanatory utility lies in an
undefined word or expression. Imagine someone asking,

'How did the universe come into existence?' and being answered, 'It was created by Fred' or 'It was created by the supreme egg.' Obviously, such a response explains nothing because it means nothing. There is no greater explanatory power or meaning if one puts 'god', 'God' or 'the supreme being' in place of 'Fred' or 'the supreme egg'.

The point is that the word 'god' is just too vaguely specified. 'Fred' differs in being somewhat better defined, given that it is known to be a male's name, mainly used by English-speaking people and short for 'Frederick' or 'Alfred'. Matters would not be better with 'supreme egg'. 'Supreme' has connotations of 'greater' in comparison to like things, though the comparative adjective 'greater' is by itself unclear unless it qualifies something – say, worth, power, height or weight. For this reason the phrase 'supreme being', like 'supreme egg', lacks a proper sense though obviously it has emotional significance for those to whom it suggests something great, even if they do not quite know what.

The last resort of the religious apologist is, familiarly, to invoke ineffability. The apologist challenged to explain what is meant by the word 'god' is apt to say that god is a mystery, too great for our finite minds to comprehend. Again familiarly, this closes down conversation, which of course is a useful result for the apologist.

But getting an account of what is meant by 'god' matters, because without one the religious apologist is himself in difficulty; the ineffability move does not help him. This is illustrated by looking at what results if one inspects the traditional attributes of deity in the light of the 'problem of natural evil'. If a god is all-loving, merciful, kind, compassionate and the like, how can it tolerate pain, misery and arbitrary suffering, independent of the merits of the sufferer? How could it create or tolerate a world that is sometimes brutal to sentient beings, in tsunamis, earthquakes, terrible diseases, violent death, terror and panic? Few human beings would inflict any of these things on those they have created (their children) or about whom they care. The existence of natural evil – disease and disaster – appears to be inconsistent with the idea of a benevolent agency, most especially if that agency designed and created such a universe.

I once had a published written debate with a religious apologist who, after I had argued the standard line that the idea of a loving and merciful deity is inconsistent with the fact of natural evil, said that this meant his god was not all-powerful, and therefore was not to blame because it could not stop natural evil occurring.[1] This is a different tack from the more robust one that says natural evil is a response to humanity's moral evil. What this latter view in effect argues is that because of (say) Hitler's wrongdoings, thousands of babies deserve to be drowned in tsunamis. The incoherence of this is doubtless why my debating opponent opted for redefining the traditional god as not omnipotent; for if it were, its failure to protect the good and the innocent from the horrors of natural evil would be a culpable matter.

An even more heroic choice for my opponent would have been to say that his god is omnipotent, but not benevolent. Thus, it created a world in which cruel sufferings are intentional. Since these are experienced by good and bad alike, and bear no relation to merit, such a deity would scarcely be worthy of praise and love.

The evidence of the world is in fact far more consistent with the existence of an evil deity than a good deity, or at least a deity capable of evil and more than occasionally intent on causing it; but this is not a line that many religious apologists take. This is the cherry-picking problem again, because the Bible gives ample ground for just such a view: Amos 3: 6 says, 'Does evil befall a city, and the Lord has not done it?' Isaiah 45: 7 says, 'I make peace and create evil; I am the Lord who does all these things.' Job 2: 10 says, 'Shall we receive good at the hand of God, and shall we not receive evil?' Scholars of theological history point out that these are early views of the deity, who by the New Testament has become perfectly good, benign and merciful – except that it is just, too, which introduces a second new tension alongside the natural evil dilemma: between justice and mercy. The victims of the Holocaust might wish to see their god extend justice rather than mercy to those who gassed their children in Auschwitz, however fine a thing forgiveness is. Are there not unforgivable things? Even the New Testament says there is one: namely, blasphemy. Some would think the murder of millions less forgivable than abusing the holy name.

Omnipotence is a problem for religious apologists for more reasons than this inconsistency with benevolence plus natural evil. Omnipotence strictly implies that anything is possible. But this cannot mean that it could do logically impossible things, like for example both existing and not existing at the same time, or being 'greater' or 'more perfect' than itself. It is not clear whether omnipotence implies that a possessor of it could do things that are not so obviously logically impossible, such as eat itself for breakfast.

It is sometimes claimed that a deity is a 'necessary' being, that is, one that must exist and cannot in any way avoid existing. This entails that it cannot do certain things that are otherwise both logically and contingently possible for other beings, such as cause itself to cease to exist (to commit suicide).

These points are intended to indicate the problems with the concept of an omnipotent being, and of a 'necessary being'. These are phrases that appear to have meaning but on examination turn out to make no sense.

Hence the last resort of the apologist, the appeal to mystery, ineffability, the finitude of the human intellect, the impossibility of our grasping what is meant. This, as already noted, is a convenient move, because it closes down conversation entirely, giving the religious apologist a 'get out of jail free' card for use any time and in any circumstances.

But it should not be allowed to do so. One reason was mentioned in the Introduction. Think of what is wrong with a contradiction – the assertion 'both x and not-x at the same time' is a simple example. Contradictions entail anything whatever. You can deduce anything from them. They license any train of thought or consequences. They are therefore useless. Contradictions defeat and frustrate clear thought and good reasoning. In similar vein, the philosopher of science Karl Popper remarked that a theory that explains everything explains nothing, because a good theory is one that specifies what would refute it; it should indicate what would constitute a test of its worth. But this is exactly what is wrong with a concept that cannot be defined or explained, cannot be tested, cannot even be understood. This is a concept that has no meaning. As such it is of course consistent with everything; it allows anything to be said, believed, claimed, asserted, denied, invoked – it is a credit card that buys anything you like, but whose use never costs you a cent.

Putting all these matters in this rather roundabout way is

unavoidable, because apologists for religion are typically apt to respond to accounts of their views, and especially to criticism of their views, by saying, 'That's not what I mean by religion,' 'That's not what I mean by God,' 'That's a caricature of what I believe,' and so on. If any such do not mean by 'religion' what has been painstakingly identified in the foregoing, then that closes the conversation: a strategy that apologists under pressure are frequently keen to adopt.

The difficulty of clarifying the belief commitments of a religious person who adopts the 'that's not what I mean' strategy is made greater when one notes the difference between what ordinary believers believe, and the sophisticated versions of doctrine found in what theologians and ecclesiastics say. Take Christianity for example. The ordinary churchgoer has a more or less vague idea of a human-like (only grander) being or more accurately beings – God the 'father', Jesus and the 'Holy Ghost'; and for certain sects of Christianity there are also, variously, the Virgin Mary, saints, angels and archangels, a devil or devils. Such people believe, or take themselves to believe, as literally true such propositions as that God became man, was born of a virgin, was killed but some days later came back to life, 'rose into heaven' (how many of them thought – or still think, though surely now without thinking about it properly – that there was an actual act of floating or flying upwards?). But if one examines the utterances of theologians one finds that, in the complexified and polysyllabic rarifications of their craft, not many of these propositions are taken literally. Instead they are interpreted metaphorically or mystically, though it is a matter of controversy as to which parts of the story are to be taken, or for doctrinal purposes must be taken, as literal truth, and which not. One controversy concerns the resurrection of

Jesus from the dead. For most Christians this is absolutely key to their entire faith. If it did not happen, or at least unless one believes it happened, the rest would seem to be empty. Yet there are theological views to the effect that the resurrection is a symbol, a complicated myth which addresses some aspect of our psychological attitude to death, or our need to 'die to ourselves and be reborn' with a new orientation to life and the world.

If the theologians' decisions about what is true and what is metaphorical are not a mere matter of convenience, based on what they are willing to believe or can bring themselves to believe, the next question is: what are the principled grounds for saying what is true and what is metaphor in the texts and traditions? The texts on which Christianity rests were until quite recently regarded as literal historical truth in their entirety. Fundamentalists still believe this. And almost all Muslims believe that the Qur'an is literal historical truth. But increasingly, in a more educated and scientific age, the frequent implausibilities and absurdities of these texts have forced theologians into explaining-away and cherry-picking. If a medieval Christian were to be resurrected today, he would scarcely recognise his religion in what he encounters in an American megachurch or an Anglican Sunday service.

Most Christians think that their religion is unique and correct. Yet the various mythologies that antedate Christianity contain many stories of gods impregnating mortal maidens who then give birth to exceptional individuals, some of whom descend into and return from the underworld and then join their father in his abode. This makes it a puzzle why anyone should regard the story of God impregnating Mary – and all the rest of the story that follows – as out of the ordinary, instead of being a rather obvious borrowing from familiar myths. Only consider Zeus, king of the gods in the Greek pantheon: he had dalliances with about thirty mortal maids and matrons, including (in alphabetical order) Alcmene, Antiope, Callisto, Danae, Electra, Europa, Io, Lamia, Leda, Niobe, Olympias and Semele. He visited them in various forms, as a shower of gold (Danae), a swan (Leda), a white bull (Europa), disguised as their husbands (Alcmene), and so imaginatively on. As a result of these adventures, these girls and women variously gave birth to Hercules, Castor and Pollux, Helen of Troy, Alexander of Macedon, Lacedaemon, Minos, Rhadamanthus, Dardanus, and a number of other salient figures of myth, legend and history.

The mythologising instinct is a far-reaching one. For a long time in antiquity Plato's admirers believed that he must have been the son of a god, and that once, when he was an infant, bees gathered on his lips while he slept, to foretell the honeyed beauty of his writings. Most of the founders of the city-states of Greece were attributed divine origins, as were almost all their heroes. How else were ancient people to explain the qualities that made some individuals outstanding, other than by giving them divine parentage?

Reflection on the historical contingencies that make some traditions survive while others fade away helps one to see that it is largely a matter of historical accident that some people today should, instead of slitting a bull's throat or pouring out libations of wine to mountain-top deities, think they are eating the body and drinking the blood of a god – this being what is claimed in the Roman Catholic doctrine of transubstantiation. The turning of bread and wine into human flesh and blood is said to be a miracle; this shows that miracles happen very many times a day, in the celebration of the Mass. This raises a question whether commonplace miracles, as nothing special, can really be miracles; and anyway they should be subject to empirical test by science. But what would the theologian say if a wafer was bread under the microscope both before and after all the prayers and invocations that the priest could utter over it? He would not take that as disproof of the mysteries of the Mass; these would remain – mysteries.

Transubstantiation ought to be a contradictory idea anyway, given that gods are not generally supposed to have physical blood-containing bodies, except in Mormonism, which teaches that even 'God the father' was once human; but faith is able to encompass anything. After all, the doctrine of transubstantiation makes the same sort of assumption as does sacrificing a bull to the gods, for this latter attributes to the gods a physical sense of smell, given that it is the savour of the roasting meat that pleases them. They so relished this aroma that when the ancients were embarking on a very great endeavour – a war, or the building of a new city – they sacrificed a hundred oxen (a 'hecatomb'), which would have been a very large part of their communal wealth, to ensure a great feast for the gods, and great gratitude from the gods therefore.

All this brings us to a relevant point in seeking a clarifying perspective on the ideas we are dealing with. The reasons that atheists give for rejecting supernaturalistic claims about the universe include why they regard the gods of Olympus, the Babylonian pantheon, the Hindu gods, and so on, as mere tales and myths. They then add that their reasons for regarding Christianity and Islam as the same kind of mythology are exactly the same. The point is sometimes put by saying that everybody is an atheist about almost all gods, the difference between true atheists and Christians or Muslims being that the latter still have one more god to go, one more god to stop believing in.

3

The Origins of Religion

Given that a powerful reason for the continuance of religion is tradition, it is relevant to think about how those traditions themselves began. This means looking beyond the legendary beginnings – the beginnings claimed by the faith traditions themselves – to the sources that can be inferred from the study of the history of ideas and from the systems of thought in contemporary stone-age societies, the latter collectively known as animism. The picture that emerges is that religion stems from the period when stories, myths and supernatural-istic beliefs served as, in effect, mankind's earliest science and technology. To the inhabitants of such a culture, natural phenomena are most intuitively explained by seeing them as the work of purposive agents who variously cause the wind to blow and the rain to fall, whose footsteps on the clouds are thunderous, and who are responsible for the cycling of the stars and the growth of vegetation in springtime. No doubt imputing agency to natural events was based by analogy on people's own experience of agency and purpose, projected onto nature. This was after all the only resource that early humans had to explain how things can be made to happen.

They could feel themselves to be causes of events, as when they threw a stone or pushed an object along the ground; how could things happen in nature unless caused, and how caused unless by an agent? It is a simple argument by analogy from their own case, and as such is an empirical argument.

Explanation and systematisation in this way amount to a kind of proto-science. Attempts to influence, propitiate or control these agencies likewise constitute a form of techno-logy, in which prayer, sacrifice and taboo are the major instruments.

If that is a conceptual genealogy of religion's origins, a kind of historical geography tracks the evolution of religion from that point onwards. Whereas the agencies or powers that made nature work were at first located in nature itself – water nymphs, dryads in trees, river and sea gods, thunder gods like Zeus and Thor – increasing knowledge about nature, and mastery of parts of it, obliged these agencies to relocate themselves first to mountain-tops (Olympus, Sinai), then to the sky – anyway, too far off for ordinary folk to see and interact with them in normal circumstances, though prophets and priests did not have these difficulties. And since then these agencies have moved beyond space and time altogether.

Most things that happen have more causes than they need – a phenomenon known as 'overdetermination' – and the roots of religion of course lie in much more than early efforts at explanation and control. Reflection suggests that this proto-science origin is actually quite a rational one – an attempt at sense-making – given the limitations that our earliest ancestors faced. But there is doubtless more to the story. We can surmise that eating hallucinogenic mushrooms, accidentally getting drunk because of fermented grains,

suffering ergot poisoning, experiencing an epileptic aura or
the delirium of fever, witnessing strange, unfamiliar, ominous-
seeming natural events, being caught in thunderstorms and
earthquakes, getting lost in dark woods, being frightened by
shadows, hearing the whispering of wind in tree tops, having
a stroke, a head injury or a brain tumour – a great palette of
things – easily gave rise to supernaturalistic beliefs in our
forebears, who supposed that in these experiences they were
encountering the supernatural, or seeing into different
realities.

We can surmise further that some individuals saw the
advantage to be gained from claiming to understand these
phenomena, and to be able to communicate with the agencies lurking within them or causing them. Or perhaps some
people – hearers of voices, maybe, now better understood in
psychiatric medicine – sincerely believed that they were in
touch with those agencies. Once a system of beliefs had
evolved, and people were convinced by them and lived
within their frames of rhetoric, it would have been easy and
natural to interpret further examples of these and other such
phenomena in the light of them.

But as the agencies premised in these beliefs and practices
moved further outward, retreating beyond the horizon of
scientific knowledge as it advanced, their usefulness to
temporal powers – kings and chieftains – often in the form
of a pragmatic relationship between rulers and priests, ensured
that the belief systems not merely survived but flourished.
History shows just how much utility there was in this symbi-
osis, because religious belief can be a powerful instrument of
social control, and was very much used as such. The institutionalisation of religion is a matter of record, and is one of
the principal reasons that religion has survived so long.

One immediate result of social reinforcement of religion is that whereas children give up their Father Christmas and Tooth Fairy beliefs as a matter of course in their maturation, religious indoctrination in childhood, and the continued observance or even just lip-service to religion in society, keeps it going.

In British schools children were once required to take weekly classes known as 'RI', which meant 'religious instruction'. Ponder the meaning of that phrase. This has now been replaced by 'RS' or 'religious studies', and in many cases this means a fairly neutral comparative introduction to the different religions of the world. In too many cases, however, 'RS' remains 'RI', not least in so-called 'faith schools' run by one or another religious community despite being funded by the general public through taxes. This could not happen in the United States of America, which is officially a secular country, where public money cannot be used to promote religious activity.

The most compelling case against 'faith schools' can be summed up in two words: Northern Ireland. The divisiveness and potential for conflict in sectarian schooling is so stark that its continued existence and even promotion is incomprehensible.

One has to ask how it is that although 'religious studies' have replaced 'religious instruction' the differences between religions are not made salient. Why is it not a major talking-point, as a result of the comparative study of religions, that the world's major religions contradict and indeed blaspheme each other, which is one main reason why our forebears frequently went to war with one another, committing the cruellest atrocities in the process? To this day it remains a conviction among votaries of any one religion that other religions – and other sects of their own religion – are wrong. If this were explored as a curriculum requirement in religious studies classes, it might have a desirably immunising effect. But it is not sufficiently explored or emphasised, because the 'respect' agenda – the assumption that religious faith automatically deserves respect – and the overriding imperative to tread lightly around the different faiths represented by the family backgrounds of the children in the classroom, continue to mask and distort plain but very important truths.

It would, though, be far better if religious doctrines and systems were not taught to people until they had attained maturity. If this were the case, how many would subscribe to a religion? Without being given a predisposition through childhood indoctrination to think there might be something in one of the many and conflicting religious beliefs on offer, the likely answer would surely be: not very many.

The religions are of course aware of this. Accordingly they exploit the fact that, for good evolutionary reasons, children are highly credulous, and believe anything that the adults in their immediate circle tell them. This is life-protecting when they are told that fire is painful to touch, that they must not go near the edge of a cliff, that they must avoid putting their fingers into electricity sockets. Equally, most of the fabric of ordinary knowledge that we use to navigate the world – what is called folk-physics and folk-psychology, that is, the day-to-day practical and framework-providing knowledge that enables us to function normally, navigate our world and interact with others – is acquired through instruction and example given by adults, which children unquestioningly absorb. In the same way they absorb those adults' religious outlooks. If the adults are themselves zealous, if they are unquestioning and enclosed in their religious outlook, such that the miracles and legends of their faith are as real as the cars passing in the street outside, the child is going to be zealous likewise, or – perhaps more often – will have its emotional work cut out later in life when confronted by doubt.

4

An Axe to the Root

The details of the different sects of each of the religions are so numerous that it takes many volumes of religious encyclopaedias to explain them. Fortunately a discussion of religion as such does not require that each variant of it be examined. Physical trees can be cut down branch by branch for practical reasons, but conceptual trees have to be cut down at the root. Accordingly it is the basis of religious belief alone that requires discussion. Often, religious apologists claim that critics of religion are ignorant of the finer points of theology and doctrine, accusing them of failing to read theology in formulating objections; but they thereby entirely miss the point that when one rejects the premises of a set of views, it is a waste of one's time to address what is built on those premises.

For example, if you conclude – on the basis of rational investigation – that your character and your fate are not determined by the apparent arrangement of the minority of planets, stars and galaxies that can be seen from Earth, then you do not need to compare classic tropical astrology with sidereal astrology, or either with the Sarjatak astrological system, or any of these three with any other astrological system. The different astrological systems are elaborate and complicated, but as they are all derived from profound and ancient ignorance about the real nature of the heavenly bodies, tackling this latter fundamental point is all that is required to show that none of the systems, however long-standing, complex and technical, merits examination.

Religion is exactly the same kind of thing as astrology: it originates in the pre-scientific, rudimentary metaphysics of our ancestors. In Europe and the world that Europe formed, in the civilisation once called Christendom, it survives – but dwindlingly: the numbers of the committed are steadily falling, though high among particular groups such as Africans and American southerners.

Among these latter groups, and in much etiolated and cherry-picked form among 'Christmas and Easter' observants, it survives for emotional, historical and institutional reasons, in most cases by constant self-reinvention to escape the intellectual censure that its earlier dogmas invite.

For example: a decision of the Anglican Church in a 1996 Synod shed the doctrine of hell as a place of eternal punishment for sinners, redescribing hell as 'the absence of God' and saying that the punishment for *very* bad people is annihilation. The devil is rarely if ever mentioned in moderate Protestant communions, though much present in the hellfire preaching of fundamentalist Christians in the US and Africa. In Africa 'witches' are persecuted and killed by Christians.

Not all the sects temporise, though. Evangelicals are not ones to pull punches. A BBC report of an evangelical document published in 2000 and called *The Nature of Hell* runs as follows – and it is worth quoting because of what else it reveals about the mindset that produced it:

The flames of hell, recently doused to a state of 'nothing-ness' by the Church of England, are to be reignited. *The Nature of Hell*, a 140-page report drawn up by the Evangelical Alliance, says that while biblical images of burning lakes should not be taken literally, they symbolise the horrors that are in store for people who reject Christian teaching.

The report, published next week, claims that sinners consigned to hell will face unimaginable torment based on the severity of sins they commit in life. Hell, according to the study, is 'a sphere of damnation, punishment, anguish and destruction'.

The Evangelical Alliance was formed in 1846, and represents Christians from all denominations, including many Anglicans. It claims to represent a million Christians, and campaigns on contemporary social issues. 'Hell is more than mere annihilation at the point of death,' it says. 'There are degrees of punishment and suffering in hell related to the severity of sins committed on Earth.'

It is at odds with a 1996 Church of England report approved by the General Synod which claimed traditional views of hell were outmoded. It said 'hell' was merely an absence of God, and that sinners were far more likely to face swift annihilation than eternal suffering.

The new study, which has been welcomed by the Roman Catholic Church, also urges church leaders not to be afraid of telling their congregations of the realities of hell.

It also calls for a greater emphasis on the teaching of hell in schools and theological colleges.

According to [a spokesperson], the new study is based on teachings in the Bible. 'We can't be absolutely sure what hell is,' he says. 'In a lot of aspects we can't know the full extent of God's grace. But Jesus had more to say about hell than any other person in the Bible. All people are initially damned to hell, which is why it was necessary for Jesus to offer an escape route to eternity. Anybody can get to Heaven, but the only way you can do that is through Jesus Christ.'[2]

A reader who passes over the implications of the claim reported here that only Christians will be saved from the torments of hell, thus condemning Jews, Muslims, Hindus and everyone else to 'horrors' and 'unimaginable torment', to 'damnation, punishment, anguish and destruction', is taking the usual line these days: hardly anyone, other than members of such organisations themselves, takes this kind of talk seriously. But it should be taken seriously enough to recognise how rebarbative and divisive it is, and how coercive it is intended to be. It is an ugly view; it tells us that we are created diseased by a certain doctor – 'All people are initially damned to hell' it says – that only this doctor has the cure, and that we must completely submit to this doctor, in continual worship, praise and obedience, in order to get the cure. The fact that people simply ignore these kinds of utterances, and pass them by with a shrug, is perverse: it allows unpleasant nonsense to persist unchallenged, and eventually a few hotheaded devotees of this view will do a lot of harm in service to it.

Roman Catholicism still forbids contraception, termination of pregnancy even in cases of rape or danger to the mother's health, and medical stem-cell research; and it condemns homosexuality. Yet the majority of its members do not agree with it on these points. This illustrates how, in its practical effects, religion so often fosters hypocrisy, as when most Catholics practise contraception despite being forbidden to do so by the church they attend on Sundays and to whose schools they send their children. The Catholic clergy contains a higher proportion of gay men and women than the general population, and it has been repeatedly shaken by child sex abuse scandals, which as an institution it has criminally attempted to conceal. Yet its moral teaching is the very opposite of what too many of its own officers and followers practise. Preaching one thing, or professing to accept that preaching, yet doing the opposite, is the definition of hypocrisy.

These remarks are made in full recognition of the fact that on both the personal and institutional levels many religious organisations carry out charitable works that do much good. That is not in question. Nor is the fact that religious piety has been the source of inspiration in art and music, as acknowledged in the Introduction. But there are two points to be made about these facts when they are offered as defences of religion. The first is that non-religious people and organisations also engage in charitable work, and do so without the strings that too often attach to religious charity. One could endlessly list examples: Oxfam, Médecins Sans Frontières, the Medical Foundation for the Victims of Torture, most NGOs registered at the United Nations, government aid agencies – a very long list indeed of secular organisations are at the forefront of charity, aid and human rights work in the world, and greatly outweigh religious charities in number and resources.

Secondly, it has to be asked whether the price paid by humanity for the charitable and artistic contributions of religion has been worth it. This is a challenging question. To put it bluntly: suppose you were asked to choose between keeping the Sistine Chapel ceiling or saving the lives of those burned to death at the stake by the Inquisition. What would you say?

Consider the following responses: first, that this is an unfair question, an artificially forced choice; or second, that a great and enduring work of art might after all be worth a large number of painful human deaths, given that those individuals were going to die anyway.

The first response will not do. The institution that commissioned the Sistine paintings from Michelangelo also ran the Inquisition and applied its sanctions. They are both expressions of that faith movement. The second response is more honest, though considerably less palatable.

The proper response is of course to say that we want the Sistine Chapel paintings and we do not want the burnings at the stake. But history has not allowed us to have our cake and eat it.

Commentators notice that people who do not have a religious commitment, but on the contrary voice their opposition to religion and its influence in the world, often sound angry and contemptuous of religion when they do so. This is indeed a tone that surfaces continually in the debate, and it is frankly a hard one to subdue, because too many inducements to both sentiments offer themselves. This relates to the way that, until the 9/11 atrocities in New York and Washington, people of overt religious commitment expected to be treated with respect, so that to challenge them, to express disagreement with them, to scorn their beliefs and practices, was regarded as at least bad manners. But the 'respect agenda' is at an end, which explains the robust nature of the challenge offered to religion, and the often acerbic tenor of the debate.

Although this is inevitable, given how high the stakes are, it should not distract from the substance of the arguments involved. The audience for the arguments is the general public, not just the committed on both sides, and the aim is to change minds and make a concrete difference. It is worth bearing in mind that a dispassionate tone might fail to communicate the urgency and importance that attaches to the debate; if so, that would be a worse failing than to allow a major world difficulty and a human rights problem to persist because opposition to it was whispered politely rather than proclaimed frankly, robustly and out loud. Polite opposition did not abolish slavery. It took arguments, campaigns and fearless outspoken criticism of the system and its fortifications. Freeing the human mind from the enslavement of superstition and religion requires the same approach. As Frederick Douglass said: 'Those who profess to favour freedom and yet depreciate agitation, are people who want crops without ploughing the ground; they want rain without thunder and lightning; they want the ocean without the roar of its many waters. The struggle may be a moral one, or it may be a physical one, or it may be both. But it must be a struggle.'[3]

5

Knowledge, Belief and Rationality

A key question in debates about religion turns on the question of knowledge. Religious apologists say that no one can know that there is no god; many people choose to describe themselves as agnostics on the grounds that there cannot be absolute certainty either way; scientists, out of respect for the essential defeasibility of knowledge (which means: there is always a chance, even if only a vanishingly tiny chance, that in regard to a particular theory or proposition we could be wrong), claim never to rule out any possibility, even that there is a china teapot orbiting Jupiter.

If I were to succeed in making only one contribution to this debate, it would be to establish the point that what is at stake in it, as indeed with every debate about any subject matter other than logic and mathematics, is not knowledge but rationality, and that 'proof' outside formal systems of logic and mathematics means 'test'; so that the only propositions we are entitled to accept as premises for action and further thought are those that it is rational to accept because they have passed the test of reason or observation or both.

To talk of knowing something – let us continue to use the term 'proposition' to denote what tells us what a knowledge-claim or belief-claim is about – is a shorthand for saying that one regards the given proposition as true, and securely capable of being used as a premise in further reasoning and action.

In all talk of contingent matters there is an assumed 'other things being equal' rider, and that what we think about contingent (empirical, non-logical) matters is always defeasible. Both are understood.

So far so good. But now consider that, familiarly, no knowledge claim can be arbitrary; it must have a justification. And if it is going to stand up to scrutiny, the justification must be good. This is where rationality enters the picture. 'Ratio' means 'proportion', so to be rational about beliefs means proportioning the evidence or grounds one has for holding that belief to the belief itself.

An example clarifies the point. Suppose I say: 'Whenever I have gone outdoors in the rain without an umbrella, I have got wet. But my belief that I will get wet next time I go out in the rain without an umbrella is merely inductive; all past instances of getting wet in the rain because I had no umbrella do not entail that this will happen next time. So I will not take an umbrella with me the next time it rains, because it is possible that I will stay dry.'

I take it as uncontroversial that anyone who reasoned in this way would be viewed as irrational. This shows that the primary mark of rationality is reliance on evidence, taking relevant experience seriously, and using associated knowledge and theory appropriately. In the umbrella case, this means applying what one knows about rain, wetness, and what an umbrella does.

Suppose you are asked whether you would bet your house on there being a china teapot orbiting Jupiter. You would not. If you were asked to bet your house on getting wet in the rain if you had no umbrella, you would. You would not hesitate in either case. The practical application of rational thought in each case is indistinguishable from *knowing* that there is not a china teapot orbiting Jupiter, and that you get wet in the rain if you do not have an umbrella.

Moreover, what we think is rational to believe and do as regards umbrellas and rain is set in a broader system of expectations, rational judgements and experience. The rationality of any given belief is a function of, among other things, the cumulative rationality of beliefs that support or challenge it.

The umbrella example relates to an ordinary contingent belief that is inductively based. In philosophical discussions of inductive reasoning one approach is to regard the justification of inductive inferences as residing in the rationality of accepting their conclusions.[4] The significance of such a view can be understood independently of whether it solves philosophy's 'traditional problem of induction', for it explains the following crucial fact: why an ordinarily rational person would answer 'No' if asked, 'Do you believe that fairies exist?' and 'Yes' if asked, 'Do you believe that water molecules exist?', rather than, 'It is more probable that water molecules exist than that fairies exist,' or, 'I attach a low probability to the existence of fairies and a high probability to the existence of water molecules.' This is an important point which merits examination, as follows.

One line of thinking in the theory of knowledge has it that belief is not an all-or-nothing affair, but a matter of degree. The degree in question can be represented as a probability value. A virtue of this approach is said to be that it explains how people adjust the weighting they give to their various beliefs as the evidence in support of them changes when more or better information becomes available. People might not talk of probabilities unless challenged to say just how strongly they believe something, but their beliefs are nevertheless measurable in terms of how subjectively probable they appear to their holder. In what is known as Bayesian probability theory this is taken to underlie all acquisition and evaluation of beliefs.

If this is right, no intellectually scrupulous individual could say, 'I do not believe that fairies exist outside children's books,' and by this quite plainly mean, 'There are no such things as fairies.' Instead he would have to say, 'I attach a very low probability to there being such things as fairies.' Yet if we met someone who thought this – that is, that it is *unlikely* that fairies exist, instead of taking it that there *are no* such things – we would not regard him as rational, but as irrational. This is because the question of whether it is rational or not to believe something is an all-or-nothing affair, and not a matter of degree. And then the ethics of rationality require that what we think it is rational to believe, we believe and act upon; and what it is irrational to believe, we reject and do not act upon.

It is of course the case that it is sometimes uncertain whether something is or is not so, because the evidence pushes both ways, or is insufficient. Then the rational course is either to suspend judgement (this is what agnostics mistakenly think they are doing; see below) or to take a chance, helped by any external considerations that give some inclining help. This typically happens when the probability in question is around 50 per cent. But it is not rational to bet on something's being the case that has a probability of 99.9 per cent of not being the case, and since acceptance of a belief is exactly comparable to taking a bet, the questions 'is it rational to bet on x' and 'is it rational to believe in x' alike admit of unequivocal yes/no answers.

The initial probability of there being a deity is not 50 per cent, as some try to argue. This is a hidden assumption of agnosticism, which premises the thought that there is insufficient evidence to settle the matter either way. One can see this by asking what initial probability should be attached to the existence of (say) dryads or unicorns, or anything else whose presence in myth, fable, legend and religion derives from what our remote ancestors handed down among their stories about the world. Whatever that probability is, if it is not 0 then it is vanishingly close to 0 – though it indeed seems odd even to say 'the probability that unicorns exist is vanishingly small'. The mistake made by many is to think that because a particular tradition has been institutionalised in society, it increases the probability that the things it talks about actually exist.

What this shows is that it is an important mistake to think that the key point about belief is probability rather than rationality. It allows religious apologists to squeeze into the tiny gap left by the point-millions-of-zeroes-one probability that the proposition 'god exists' – whatever this proposition means – might be true, and to take that as enough of a reason to be believers. This is what Pascal did in his 'wager' (see pp. 99–103).

Whether with respect to some matters it is rational to disbelieve and therefore act accordingly, rational to believe and therefore act accordingly, or rational to suspend judgement and either not act or act in whatever prudential way seems best on ancillary grounds, is a clear-cut matter in each case. In connection with fairies, deities and unicorns, the clear option is the first: for the following reasons.

The considerations that give weight to our ordinary beliefs and choices derive from common experience, applied and practical endeavour, and organised scientific investigation. The second category, applied endeavour, can be described as the expertise which has accumulated historically in the way of farming techniques, construction of buildings, medical practice and so on, and what they have taught us about the world.

In the first two cases the responsible norm, and in the case of science the professional norm, is that what we think and do must be proportioned to the available evidence, which includes the long-term outcomes of trial and error in the first two cases and the disciplined, public and repeatable outcome of experiments and testing in the case of science.

In each of these fields there are norms that specify what counts as evidence, what counts as a test of the evidence, what constitutes support for or challenge to hypotheses, and how much confidence can be placed in conclusions arrived at. Different fields of enquiry impose different requirements, but the collective endeavour in each defines what it is rational to accept. The paradigm is science, which institutionalises publicity, repeatability and peer-review of experiment and test.

The views and practices that emerge from common sense, practicality and science form a general picture of a law-like natural realm in which we know what it is rational to believe and do, and what it is not. For example: we know that it is rational to expect that we can heat and light our houses by installing the right kinds of appliances and connecting them to a power source, and simultaneously we know that it is irrational to believe that we can light and heat our houses by prayer or by sacrificing an ox.

This is exactly why it is rational to believe the deliverances of common sense, practicality and science, and irrational to believe religious claims. The former are based on evidence gathered and vastly confirmed by experience, whereas the beliefs of the various religions are untestable, inconsistent with each other, internally contradictory, and in conflict with the deliverances of common sense and science.

Some who wish to make room for two 'magisteria' repudiate this last remark, by arguing that religion and science address and operate in wholly different spheres, and therefore do not compete and cannot be compared. Unfortunately for the apologists, this attempt will not work. Religions make claims that certain entities exist in or attached to the universe, and further claim that this fact has a significant impact on the universe or at least on humans on this planet. If these claims have content, they should be testable. Yet they are untestable, and at sharp odds with everything that science and common sense shows us about the nature of reality.

In fact religion and science are competitors for the truth about quite a number of things, including the origins of the universe, the nature of human beings, and the belief that the laws of nature can be locally and temporarily suspended – thus allowing for miracles. We can be confident that if tests were arranged to adjudicate between these competing claims, they would be won by science. Religious apologists have a convenient escape clause, however; they can always quote the scripture that says, 'God will not be tested.'

To illustrate these points it is sufficient to contrast current theory in geology and biology with belief in a six-day creation that occurred six thousand years ago. Geology and biology construct theories on the basis of observation, experiment and reason, and these theories themselves specify what would count as counter-evidence to them when tested. If a religion specified what would testably show it to be false, it would have the same standing. This is a key matter, for it relates to Karl Popper's point that a theory which explains everything – which is consistent with anything and everything – explains nothing. Religious claims are, accordingly, irrefutable because untestable; and by this criterion are therefore meaningless.

6

Agnosticism, Atheism and Proof

No doubt the convinced apologist for religion will resist the last chapter's claim that demonstrating the irrationality of religious belief is enough to overturn his view, on the putative grounds that even if one can prove that it is irrational to accept religious beliefs, this does not prove that they are false. Historical examples leap to his defence: it was once rational for our forebears to believe that the Earth is flat, but they were ultimately proved wrong. The apologist takes comfort from the nanometre of possibility that appears to be left open by this, and regards it as enough to have faith that however irrational religious belief might be, nevertheless one can believe. (It is a problem for the apologist that this licenses continued belief in the Earth's being flat: and it equally supports non-belief in religious claims.)

But there is an answer even to this, and a good way of illustrating it is to examine a concession made by a famous opponent of religion, Bertrand Russell, when he described himself as an 'agnostic' for precisely the religious apologist's reason.

Russell's own definition of the term 'agnostic' shows what is meant. In the article 'What is an Agnostic?' he said: 'An agnostic is a man who thinks it is impossible to know the truth in matters such as God and future life with which the Christian religion and other religions are concerned, or, if not for ever impossible, at any rate impossible at present.'

He then proceeds to define 'atheist':

Are agnostics atheists? No. An atheist, like a Christian, holds that we *can* know whether or not there is a God. The Christian holds that we can know there is a God, the atheist that we can know there is not. The agnostic suspends judgment, saying that there are not sufficient grounds either for affirmation or for denial. At the same time, an agnostic may hold that the existence of God, though not impossible, is very improbable; he may even hold that it is so improbable that it is not worth consider-ing in practice. In that case, he is not far removed from atheism. His attitude may be that which a careful philoso-pher would have towards the gods of ancient Greece. If I were asked to *prove* that Zeus and Poseidon and Hera and the rest of the Olympians do not exist, I should be at a loss to find conclusive arguments. An agnostic may think the Christian God as improbable as the Olympians; in that case he is, for practical purposes, at one with the atheists.[5]

This latter, then, was what Russell meant by calling himself an agnostic: he was 'at one with the atheists' but felt bound by logic to admit that he would be at a loss to find arguments to disprove the existence of the Olympian deities.

Russell's view merits challenge. As a logician who, in the decades after the publication of *Principia Mathematica*, devoted so much effort to showing how science, as (to use his terminology) knowledge by description, can be derived ultimately from knowledge by acquaintance (meaning observation and experiment), he should have distinguished between proof in a formal deductive system (demonstrative proof) and proof in the empirical setting (scientific proof).

The former – demonstrative proof – consists in deriving a conclusion from premises by rules, and is literally an *explication* in the sense that all the information constituting the conclusion already exists in the premises, so a derivation is in fact a rearrangement. There is no logical novelty in the conclusion, though often enough there is psychological novelty, in the sense that the conclusion can seem unobvious or even surprising if the information constituting it was highly dispersed among the premises.

Demonstrative proof is watertight and conclusive. It is a mechanical matter; computers do it best. Change the rules or axioms of a formal system, and you change the results. Such proof is only to be found in logic and mathematics.

Proof in all other spheres of enquiry, and paradigmatically in science, consists in adducing evidence of the kind and in the quantity that makes it irrational, absurd, irresponsible or even a mark of insanity to reject the conclusion thus being supported.

The definitive illustration of what this means, not least for the use that theists would like to make of the myth that 'you cannot prove a negative', is Carl Sagan's 'The Dragon in My Garage' story:

'A fire-breathing dragon lives in my garage.'
    Suppose I seriously make such an assertion to you. Surely you'd want to check it out, see for yourself. There

have been innumerable stories of dragons over the centuries, but no real evidence. What an opportunity!

'Show me,' you say. I lead you to my garage. You look inside and see a ladder, empty paint cans, an old tricycle – but no dragon.

'Where's the dragon?' you ask.

'Oh, she's right here,' I reply, waving vaguely. 'I neglected to mention that she's an invisible dragon.'

You propose spreading flour on the floor of the garage to capture the dragon's footprints.

'Good idea,' I say, 'but this dragon floats in the air.'

Then you'll use an infrared sensor to detect the invisible fire.

'Good idea, but the invisible fire is also heatless.'

You'll spray-paint the dragon and make her visible.

'Good idea, but she's an incorporeal dragon and the paint won't stick.'

And so on. I counter every physical test you propose with a special explanation of why it won't work.

Now, what's the difference between an invisible, incorporeal, floating dragon who spits heatless fire and no dragon at all? If there's no way to disprove my contention, no conceivable experiment that would count against it, what does it mean to say that my dragon exists? Your inability to invalidate my hypothesis is not at all the same thing as proving it true. Claims that cannot be tested, assertions immune to disproof are veridically worthless, whatever value they may have in inspiring us or in exciting our sense of wonder. What I'm asking you to do comes down to believing, in the absence of evidence, on my say-so . . .

Now another scenario: Suppose it's not just me. Suppose that several people of your acquaintance, including people who you're pretty sure don't know each other, all tell you that they have dragons in their garages – but in every case the evidence is maddeningly elusive. All of us admit we're disturbed at being gripped by so odd a conviction so ill-supported by the physical evidence. None of us is a lunatic. We speculate about what it would mean if invisible dragons were really hiding out in garages all over the world, with us humans just catching on. I'd rather it not be true, I tell you. But maybe all those ancient European and Chinese myths about dragons weren't myths at all.

Gratifyingly, some dragon-size footprints in the flour are now reported. But they're never made when a sceptic is looking. An alternative explanation presents itself. On close examination it seems clear that the footprints could have been faked. Another dragon enthusiast shows up with a burnt finger and attributes it to a rare physical manifestation of the dragon's fiery breath. But again, other possibilities exist. We understand that there are other ways to burn fingers besides the breath of invisible dragons. Such 'evidence' – no matter how important the dragon advocates consider it – is far from compelling. Once again, the only sensible approach is tentatively to reject the dragon hypothesis, to be open to future physical data, and to wonder what the cause might be that so many apparently sane and sober people share the same strange delusion.[6]

Someone who on the basis of evidence and reasoning concludes that it is irrational, absurd, irresponsible or even lunatic to believe that there is such a thing as dragons, or a deity, might further ask whether it is nevertheless none of these things to believe that there *might* be a deity. Consider our umbrella example again. Is the belief that 'rain might not wet me next time I do not have an umbrella' less irrational or absurd than the belief that rain does not wet at all? Obviously not. For this reason Russell's choice of 'agnostic' to describe his position is seen to turn on an assimilation of proof concerning matters of fact to proof of the demonstrative kind – and it is a quibble that does not, *pace* our man with the umbrella, hold water.

Pointing this out matters because misapprehensions about the nature of proof alone support the apparent plausibility of agnosticism. But agnosticism, as the position that entertains the possibility that there *might be* or *could be* one or more supernatural agencies of some sort, is an irrational position, for precisely the same reason as holding that there *might be* or *could be* fairies or goblins or the Olympian deities or the Norse gods. For this reason Russell on his own grounds ought to have recognised that he was entitled to declare himself an atheist, just as he was entitled by argument to announce that he was not a Christian. (And indeed, at times he did indeed describe himself as an atheist, as when, in a wry remark in his autobiography where he talks about nearly dying from pneumonia in China in 1921, he writes, 'I was told that the Chinese said they would bury me in the Western Lake and build a shrine to my memory. I regret that this did not happen, as I might have become a god, which would have been very *chic* for an atheist.')

The last word on these matters surely belongs to W. K. Clifford, writing on the 'ethics of belief':

It is wrong always, everywhere, and for anyone, to believe anything upon insufficient evidence. If a man, holding a belief which he was taught in childhood or persuaded of afterwards, keeps down and pushes away any doubts which arise about it in his mind, purposely avoids the reading of books and the company of men that call into question or discuss it, and regards as impious those questions which cannot easily be asked without disturbing it – the life of that man is one long sin against mankind.[7]

7

Theistic Arguments

In this and the following chapters I examine 'arguments for the existence of God', as the standard phrase has it. I do it in detail, and in the context of other considerations that arise in discussion of these arguments – semantic, psychological and polemical considerations chief among them – something that is too rarely done, although doing it brings a great deal of light to bear on the arguments themselves.

The importance of this contextual approach to these arguments is that apologists for religion wish to sustain the impression that such discussions are rational in the way that discussion of genetics or Roman history is rational, and in the way that discussion of fairy lore, or astrological concepts as employed in assertions such as 'Mercury is in opposition to Mars in the Third House', is not. It is rational to discuss the fact that lots of people believe that astrology reveals character and destiny, but it is not rational to discuss whether people born under the sign of Aries are typically more rash than those born under the sign of Gemini. Theological discourse is of this latter type – 'Is the Son of one substance with the Father?' and 'Does the Holy Ghost proceed from the Father and the Son, or from the Father alone?' are utterances that have caused wars, persecutions, schisms and burnings at the stake; and they are exactly of the same category as 'Are Aries people more rash than Gemini people?' – that is, they are part of the internal discourse of the belief system, and they only make sense to anyone who has accepted the premises and parameters of the belief system already.

Let us call discussion about why people believe in astrology an 'external discussion' and discussion about the different character traits of Aries and Gemini people an 'internal discussion'. We then see that 'arguments for the existence of God' are intended as external discussions, and therefore an invitation to rational argument about theistic claims. One large problem with this, as we shall repeatedly see, is that to have this external discussion one has to make use of internal discussions in the crucial sense that it is these latter which tell us what the former are about. The question is: what is this thing theists call 'god' that these arguments are going to try to prove exists? How can you prove such a thing exists (or: such things exist) unless you know what is under discussion? You can only say what is talked about by reference to the internal discussions; but the internal discussions only make sense if the external discussion has shown that there is something to talk about.

This problem has to be borne in mind throughout what follows.

Anyone who studies philosophy or theology immediately meets with a standard set of 'arguments for the existence of God'. The best known is the 'argument from design', called by philosophers the 'teleological argument' from the Greek word *telos* meaning 'aim, end or purpose'.

The second well-known argument students meet with is the 'ontological argument', an argument that claims to establish the existence of a deity by reason alone. It does this by claiming that a deity exists by definition.

A third argument is the 'cosmological argument', like the teleological argument an attempt to provide an empirical basis for the existence of a deity, but this time inferring it from the supposed fact that the world cannot be its own cause or 'ground'.

Other arguments include a moral argument, roughly speaking that there cannot be morality unless there is a deity, and a collection of further considerations intended to establish that theistic belief is rational, desirable, or at very least prudent.

In all these cases an argument is being offered, and arguments invite rational scrutiny. The word 'argument' is here being used in its logical sense to mean the derivation of a conclusion from premises. Premises can support a conclusion either demonstratively and conclusively, as in the formal deductive systems of logic and mathematics, or by rendering the conclusion plausible or persuasive to the point of making it irrational not to accept it (and, if relevant, to act upon it). This distinction was explained earlier. Argument of the latter kind is inductive. Arguments endeavouring to establish the 'existence of God' can be either deductive or inductive.

I put 'scare' quotes around the phrase 'existence of God' because, as noted earlier, use of the capitalised word 'God' makes it look like a proper name which, in virtue of being one, carries the suggestion that it names something. There is a major debate in philosophy about naming, which we know cannot have straightforward existential implications given that some names, such as 'Harry Potter', name fictional entities; and this alerts us to the possibility of question-begging assumptions being involved in arguments that claim to establish the existence of something when talking about that something already seems to presuppose its existence, or at very least the possibility of its existence.

It is better to insist on the formula I began with, namely, 'arguments for the existence of deity', although we immediately find ourselves in need of an understanding of what is meant by 'deity' or 'god' and their cognates. The difficulties relating to this, mentioned earlier, greatly complicate the task of analysing attempted proofs of existence, for how can one prove the existence of something unless one knows what it is supposed to be?

There is a further complication. This is that most religious people do not, of course, subscribe to their religion because of arguments in favour of it, still less arguments establishing the existence of the deity central to it. The arguments examined here are without exception rationalisations of beliefs which are already accepted. In the great majority of cases, people belong to their religion because it is the religion of their parents, learned in childhood and thereafter constantly and in diverse ways reinforced by being present and observed in their communities. When a religion is adopted in later years the impulse for it is almost wholly emotional rather than rational; proselytising of teenagers and adults typically targets loneliness, confusion, failure, grief, anxiety and depression as opportunities for conversion. The psychological support given by the fellowship thus offered is attributed by the convert to his newly formed relationship with that religion's deity – or so the sceptical observer of this phenomenon would say. It is difficult to find sound empirical data on the length of time that converts remain converted; anecdotal evidence suggests that late conversion, even when it produces the zeal that makes converts more devoted than the (so to speak) natives of the faith, more often than not does not 'stick'.

Because non-rational motivation plays a much greater role in prompting and supporting religious commitment than 'arguments for God's existence', it merits particular challenge, because *having faith* – holding beliefs and accepting doctrines either without evidence or even in the face of countervailing evidence, which most religious people actually regard as a virtue – directly controverts canons of intellectual integrity. 'Faith' is not a respectable or admirable thing; having been so long paraded as a virtue and worthy of respect, the truth is otherwise: its critics have no compunction in saying that it is irresponsible, lazy and too often dangerous.

Because it would be fruitless to attempt proof of the existence of something which is undefined, ineffable, or too mysterious for finite minds to understand or describe, one has constantly to remind oneself of the difficulty in attaching meaning to the word 'god' or 'deity' in talking of arguments for the existence of such a thing. As noted in Chapter 2, it is common for religious apologists to reply to critiques of such arguments by claiming that deity is incomprehensible, which puts an end to the debate because, tautologously, there is nothing to be said about what nothing can be said about. Yet as it happens, religious apologists actually find a lot to say about such a thing after all – not just that it exists, but that it has a specifiable nature (it is 'love', it is omniscient, omnipotent, morally pure and the like), and they even know with a great deal of precision what it requires of mankind in the way of behaviour and commitments. This does not appear to strike apologists as contradictory, which it is. The ineffability claim is inconsistent with the fact that most religions have scriptures or literatures which say a great deal about the divine being or beings that figure in them. The standard arguments for the existence of deity draw upon this material. For example, the classic version of the ontological argument premises that the deity whose existence it seeks to prove possesses 'all perfections', meaning at very least no limits to or defect in any such positive property as wisdom, purity and goodness (the opposites of ignorance, lustfulness and evil). The positive properties are said to include power – indeed, all-power: omnipotence – but power cannot be a positive property unless qualified as such, because presumably evil agencies (the devil and his minions) have some degree of power – they cannot work their evil otherwise. However: the all-good, pure, all-powerful, all-wise being is the tradi-tional conception of deity in the Judaeo-Christian tradition, of which there are offshoots including Islam and Mormonism; and the concept of deity in all these is therefore similar.

Note that the positive characteristics attributed to deity are the ones we humans most approve of and wish we had. Obviously enough we are finite beings, limited both in intel-ligence and in knowledge, and given to various weaknesses and failings. Our lives are brief and often beset with trouble and illness. Deities tend to have the opposite of these things, and the promise held out to those who will obey their priests is that they will achieve the same at some future time – after death usually, though some sects are more optimistic. Traditional definitions of deity turn on negations of the human lot, and are therefore anthropomorphic in reverse: based on desirable opposites of undesirable human character-istics. Those who say that the nature of deity is ineffable avoid having these considerations offered as a count against theism, but then ineffabilitists are strictly speaking not in a position to offer proofs for the existence of deity, or (more weakly) reasons why anyone might think there is any such thing: if they are serious about the ineffability claim, they have painted themselves into the corner of not being able to say very much, or indeed anything.

This raises an interesting point. Think of trying to get an investor to put money into a scheme which cannot be described or talked about. It is unlikely that anyone was ever persuaded to believe in a we-know-not-what; an indescribable deity has to be arrived at by retreat from a defined deity, a deity of tradition or childhood. The other alternative is that the person persuading someone to believe in a we-know-not-what would have to have great charisma and plausibility; no doubt this sometimes happens. But even here there has to be something to start with, some sense of the word 'god', which the persuader can say is not correctly understood (by all the other religions no doubt) or 'cannot be spoken of or described'.

The standard arguments for the existence of deity are said to belong to what is known as 'natural theology' rather than revealed religion, but we see from the foregoing considerations that what natural theology owes revealed religion in the way of a concept of deity is obvious and inescapable. Therefore it is the deity of tradition – eternal, omnipotent, omniscient, morally perfect, in short infinitely possessed of all the positive characteristics that people most admire and wish they had – whose existence the arguments for the existence of deity attempt to prove. This type of deity is to be understood as the subject under discussion throughout the following.

Another point that has to be mentioned in order to be set aside is that the deity of tradition is always referred to as 'he' (believers write 'He'); this is an accident of history, but in personalising the deity it once again forces a circular assumption that such a thing exists even in the process of attempting to prove its existence.

The two most often discussed arguments are the 'teleological' and the 'ontological'. I begin with them, taking each in turn.

8

Arguing by Design

Proponents of the teleological argument deduce the existence of a deity from the appearance of design in nature. Strictly speaking, the argument is only entitled to try proving the existence of a designer; it is a bigger step to say that this agency created the universe as well as designed it, because however natural it might be to think that an agency capable of designing a universe might also be capable of creating it, nevertheless there is no evidence in the appearance of design that the designer was the creator too.

But grant, for a moment, that if there were a designer, it would also be the creator; it is an even bigger step to get from there to the deity of a particular religious tradition, such as the Judaeo-Christian tradition. There are many other religions and mythologies in which the agency credited with creating the universe has no further interest in it, or at least no interest in humans.

Contemporary 'Intelligent Design' (ID) advocates are careful not to say what they take the teleological argument to prove the existence of, other than an Intelligent Designer – at least not while they are trying to get their textbooks into

American schools alongside biology textbooks. Their creationist or 'Creation Science' predecessors were less careful,
stating straight out that they took the argument to establish
the existence of the Judaeo-Christian 'God of the Bible'. As
the foregoing consideration shows, ID advocates would have
a task to advance beyond an Intelligent Designer if their
eventual aim – as everyone knows it is – is to defend a traditional Judaeo-Christian commitment. (Islam is a creationist
religion and faces the same problem.)

Many of those in the eighteenth century who today would
call themselves atheists described themselves as 'deists' because
they were unable to see how the universe and life could
begin without a creative act of some kind.[8] They were
puzzled by the obvious difficulty that positing a creating
agency merely pushes the problem back a step – where did
the creating agency pop up from? what explains *it*? – yet in
the absence of any other resource they accepted the fudge.
Note that this is not the same thing as an argument from
design, but rather is a version of the argument that says: 'in
the absence of having any clue as to what the explanation
might be for something, just settle for saying "a god did it".'
This is the 'god of gaps' move.

The deists also held, on the sound empirical evidence
otherwise available to them, that the creating agency was no
longer at work in the universe – that it was either no longer
around or no longer interested. Consequently they did not
subscribe to any religious practices other than for form's sake.
At that time it was, in social terms, very difficult not to pay
lip-service to the forms.

As the deists' dilemma shows, the teleological argument
was taken seriously in the eighteenth century, by which time
two centuries of science had proceeded far enough to reveal

many of the natural world's beautiful complexities, but not far enough to explain their origin and development.

The most famous statement of the argument from design was given by William Paley. In his *Natural Theology* (1802) he invites us to imagine finding a watch on the ground while out for a walk, and being forced to conclude from an examination of its structure and properties that it was made by an intelligent agent. But if we think this of a watch, which gives every indication of being wrought by a purposeful agent, how much more so must we think the same of the eye, which, he wrote, 'would be alone sufficient to support the conclusion which we draw from it, as to the necessity of an intelligent Creator'.

If this is the most intuitive statement of the design argument, the clearest statement of its logical structure is given by David Hume in his posthumously published *Dialogues Concerning Natural Religion* (1779). He has his character Cleanthes say:

> Look round the world; contemplate the whole and every part of it: You will find it to be nothing but one great machine, subdivided into an infinite number of lesser machines, which again admit of subdivisions to a degree beyond what human senses and faculties can trace and explain. All these various machines, and even their most minute parts, are adjusted to each other with an accuracy which ravishes into admiration all men who have ever contemplated them. The curious adapting of means to ends, throughout all nature, resembles exactly, though it much exceeds, the productions of human contrivance; of human design, thought, wisdom, and intelligence. Since, therefore, the effects resemble each other, we are led to

infer, by all the rules of analogy, that the causes also resemble; and that the Author of Nature is somewhat similar to the mind of man, though possessed of much larger faculties, proportioned to the grandeur of the work which he has executed. By this argument *a posteriori*, and by this argument alone, do we prove at once the existence of a Deity, and his similarity to human mind and intelligence.

Hume rejected this argument. His rejection of it turns on three points: on the weak and misleading nature of the analogy between natural things and man-made machines; on the fact that there are alternative explanations of how natural phenomena came to be as they are; and − the point made above − that if the argument established that the universe must have been designed, the most this could establish is the existence of a designer.

In accepting this last point the deists were of course being persuaded by the supposed analogy in play. But they were also making use of the fundamental principle that everything has a cause. Philosophical thinking about causation was influenced by Aristotle's doctrine of causation, which turns on a fourfold distinction between the 'formal', 'material', 'final' and 'efficient' causes of things. The 'formal cause' is the plan or design of something. The 'material cause' is the stuff out of which it is made. The 'final cause' is the purpose or end for which it came into existence. And the 'efficient cause' is the actual work that brought it about. On the analogy proposed by the teleological argument, just as intelligence ineliminably figures in any account of the final and efficient causes of human artefacts, so a like intelligence must be supposed to explain the final and efficient causes of natural things.

The weakness of this analogy, however, is revealed by the second counter offered by Hume. This is that there are other and better explanations of natural phenomena. Although cosmology and biology had not reached the levels of explanatory power that experimental and theoretical advances have since together permitted, Hume could see that postulating a designer to explain the appearance of nature blunts Ockham's Razor, the principle which states that one must employ the fewest assumptions and invoke the least number of entities necessary to explain something. So if there could be alternative explanations which are simpler in themselves and more consistent with observed fact, invoking an extra agency is unnecessary. If Ockham's Razor were not a principle of enquiry, why not hypothesise that flowers are coaxed out of their seeds and up through the soil by fairies, one for each flower?

Moreover the design hypothesis is implausible because it purports to offer an explanation by invoking something itself unexplained. The deists who felt disquiet about this should have taken their disquiet seriously, because explaining something by something unexplained amounts, obviously, to no explanation at all.

And finally the argument is inconsistent with the many examples of bad design that nature offers us (wisdom teeth and the human appendix merely begin a very long list), together with nature's failures (most life that has ever been on Earth is now extinct) and repeated efforts at producing structures (there are nearly two dozen different evolutionary pathways to types of eyes, something Paley did not know). The first point is a logical point, the second is an empirical one.

One way that defenders of the teleological argument seek to salvage it is by saying that the deity works indirectly, by making natural laws the instrument for realising his designs. He creates the laws, then the laws create nature, thus fulfilling his purposes. This however is an even worse violation of Ockham's Razor; it accepts that natural laws create the universe by themselves, and then postulates an additional entity to be a creator of the laws.

This is also an example of what Karl Popper meant when he said that a theory which is consistent with everything – which says that nothing can refute it – explains nothing. Consider the ID proponent who rejects the theory of biological evolution while arguing that the designer works through natural laws. He moves the designer further back down the causal chain so that no example of naturally occurring adaptation is inconsistent with this hypothesis – which therefore makes the hypothesis empty.

A more contemporary form of teleological argument turns on the idea of 'cosmic fine-tuning'. This argument begins from the observation that the universe's initial conditions, and the physical laws and parameters operative within it, are 'fine-tuned' in such a way as to make it possible for life to appear on this planet. Had they been different in even the smallest way, life as we know it could not have happened.

For example: if the strong force in the atomic nucleus had varied in either direction by more than 5 per cent, or if the electromagnetic force binding electrons to atomic nuclei were stronger or weaker, life could not have emerged. If the relative masses of neutrons and protons were different, life could not have emerged. If the gravitational force were different even by a minute amount, main sequence stars like our own sun could not exist and accordingly life of our kind would be much less likely.

If the 'big bang' had not been exactly as it was, either the universe would have collapsed upon itself immediately, or it would have expanded too rapidly for the evolution of stars like our sun; so either there could have been no planet Earth with life on it, or at very least our kind of life would not have appeared.

The concurrence of these just-right values constitutes what has been called 'the Goldilocks enigma'. How can the universe be so extraordinarily apt for life to emerge on our planet, given the infinitesimal chance that nature's laws should all coincide in the right way for it? Therefore – some say – it must have been designed by a purposive agency.

Much might be said in response. We are asked to think that there is an agency whose aim was to produce us by bringing it about that, after nine billion years or so – the universe is about thirteen billion years old – forms of life would emerge that after a further four billion years would eventuate in us (the first prokaryotes appeared on our planet about that long ago).

Let us leave aside the fact that this speculation makes us the aim of the great universal story; all those billions of years, billions of galaxies, billions of stars – it is all aimed at producing us, with our wars, our dentistry needs, our fashion sense. Even if these things were part of the design to test us so that we can get into another universe – the posthumous one – it would seem a trifle excessive. The least one can say is that it is a view that does not suffer from modesty about the importance of human beings to the cosmos.

Consider instead the following fact. If my great-great-great-great-grandparents (all 64 of them, living about two hundred years ago) had not lived where they did, and done the things they did – and pretty exactly as they did them – I would not exist. But this is a retrospective observation, which I can only make because in fact I exist, even if I am filled with wonder at the (very fortunate for me) millions of coincidences which resulted in me. If my forebears had been inconsiderate enough to do other things in other ways and places instead, with the result that I did not exist, I would not now be marvelling at how fine-tuned history was in bringing it about that I exist. I do not however think that my existence was the point and purpose of all these events, however lucky for me. Rather, I think that it is only because I exist that I see that I would not have existed unless these coincidences occurred.

The 'Goldilocks dilemma' of my personal existence, and that of the universe's parameters and laws, is exactly the same thing.

A variant explanation of the illusion of purpose in the 'fine-tuning' version of the design argument is provided by Voltaire's Dr Pangloss in *Candide*, a book prompted by the 100,000 deaths in the earthquake and tsunami which devastated Lisbon in 1755. The catastrophe made Voltaire doubt that this world is the 'best of all possible worlds', or that it is under the government of a benevolent agency.

Consider Dr Pangloss's explanation of the human nose, which is that it was purposely designed to support spectacles. This exposes the fallacy in the fine-tuning argument, to see which one needs to know a little logical technicality, as follows.

The fact that a human nose (use the letter X to symbolise the nose) is a *necessary condition* for spectacles to be perched in front of the eyes (use the letter Y to symbolise 'spectacles being perched in front of the eyes') does not entail that, because Y is the case, X is in itself *necessary*. 'Necessity' in the logical sense of 'having to be so' is not the same thing as the necessity involved in a 'necessary condition' – here things have to be so only *relative to* something else's being the way it is. In the case of X's being a *necessary condition relative* to Y, but not *in itself necessary*, X could have been different, and if it were so, there would, or at least might, be no Y. For example: if humans did not have noses, spectacles might be worn as goggles are, held before the eyes by an elastic strap.

This is just how it is with the universe. We humans are the Y of which nature's parameters are the X. We exist because the parameters are as they are; had they been different, we would not be here to know it. The fact that we exist because of how things happen to be with the universe's structure and properties entails nothing about design or purpose. Depending on your point of view, it is just a lucky or unlucky result of how things happen to be. The universe's parameters are not tuned *on purpose for us to exist*. It is the other way round: we exist because the laws happen to be as they are.

9

Arguing by Definition

The various versions of the *ontological argument* come down to saying in effect that deity exists by definition. It is an *a priori* deductive argument, that is, an argument by reason alone, and it turns on analysis of the concept of deity. This, therefore, is where the problems with defining the word 'god' really bite.

The classic statement of the ontological argument is given by the eleventh-century philosopher St Anselm in his *Proslogion*. He began by considering the concept of 'a being than which no greater can be conceived'. If such a being did not exist, then there would be a 'greater' being than it, namely, one that did exist. But by hypothesis 'the being than which no greater can be conceived' is the greatest being there is. Therefore, it must exist. And Anselm identified this being as the deity, because of the other attributes of deity which together make it the only plausible candidate for the 'greatest being' – omnipotence, omniscience and the rest.

Leaving aside the undefined notion of 'greatness' for a moment, let us note the following. At any given moment, someone is the tallest person in London. This is a matter of logic, not of human physiology. If there are two, three or more tallest people in London who are exactly the same height, then whichever of them got out of bed latest on the day in question would be the tallest person in London, because gravity would have had slightly longer to act on the other two, shortening them fractionally. This latter fact is a matter of physiology and physics, but it connects to the logical fact that one of the Londoners − the richest, laziest or least healthy of them, because longest abed − is the tallest on that day. Finally, note that even if everyone in London were short, as a matter of logic one of them would nevertheless be the tallest.

Now consider the idea that someone is the 'greatest' person in London. Whatever that might mean, note that such a person need not be very great, he need only be less un-great than everyone else in London. One can now see why the Anselm argument does not get us from logic to divinity. If by 'god' Anselm means the least un-great individual anywhere, this is an uninteresting result. It does not improve matters to substitute the phrase 'most perfect being' for 'greatest being', as some do with the ontological argument. The universe's most perfect being might be very imperfect, only less so than other imperfect beings, and not at all a suitable candidate for existence as a deity.

Note that the argument requires the comparative element; that is crucial; the claim cannot be 'that there is a perfect being', it must be 'that there is a most perfect being' or 'that there is a being than which no other being is more perfect', so that it can be more perfect than a perfect being which does not exist.

From the outset therefore there is the problem of getting from the supposed fact that something must have some property in the highest degree relative to any other similar thing, with it being the case that the highest degree is very high; and so without offering any ground for thinking that because it is the 'most-est' of its kind, it is a deity – let alone the traditionally conceived God.

It should also be noted, as a footnote, that there is a problem with the assumption made by proponents of some versions of the ontological argument that 'perfection' admits of degrees, making it a relative rather than an absolute notion. But there is a strong case for saying that 'perfect' is an absolute term, that is, applies in an all-or-nothing way. If something is perfect, then it is perfect, and cannot be more or less perfect than another perfect thing. It is legitimate to say that something might approach more nearly to perfection than other things do, but then by hypothesis none of the things being thus compared is perfect anyway. Yet the Anselm-type of ontological argument requires that perfection (or in Anselm's terminology, greatness) be a matter of degree, otherwise the argument will not work.

Perhaps the ontological argument's proponents take perfection to be a relative notion because it is an all too familiar fact that *imperfection* has degrees; not only are some things more imperfect than others, they can also become more and less so. But to say that something is less imperfect than something else is not to say that it is more perfect than it. It might be less imperfect in having one less flaw, and yet be extremely flawed.

The fact that 'less imperfect' is not the same as 'more perfect' is a function of the fact that the conceptual polarities 'perfect-imperfect' (and others like it, such as 'mortal-immortal') are mistakenly assimilated to such examples as 'flat-bumpy' and 'calm-anxious'. In these latter cases we know what each of the contrasting concepts applies to; we can point out examples of flat things and examples of bumpy things. But in the case of 'perfect–imperfect' and 'mortal–immortal' we only know what one of the pair applies to (imperfection and mortality, of course). The opposite pole in each case is merely notional, arrived at by extrapolation from the concept we know how to apply.

So there is a problem with the Anselm type of ontological argument which relies on an existing something's being more perfect than a non-existing perfect thing. Yet even if one leaves aside the question whether 'perfect' is an absolute or relative term, there is still a further problem. What does 'perfect' mean, as applied to deity? The formula 'God is perfect' in traditional theistic doctrine is intended to mean 'omnipotent, omniscient, morally pure, without needs or appetites' (though capable, according to the Bible, of emotions of anger and love). Arguably, though, these fall into the category of expressions which are sayable without being thinkable, like the example, given previously (p. 21), of the apparently intelligible sentence which expresses a logical impossibility.

For consider: 'omnipotent' means 'all powerful' in the sense of 'is capable of doing anything' or 'is unlimited in action'. This immediately causes difficulties, well illustrated by nonsense questions such as, 'Could an omnipotent being eat itself?' Suppose the reply is that such a being is not the kind of being that eats, because it is immaterial. Does this mean that it cannot eat? If so it is not omnipotent: omnipotent means 'can do anything'. If the answer is that it can eat but does not, then one can probe the coherence of the concept by asking, 'What might it eat if it chose to?' Alternatively, and more consistently, the first answer might be developed as follows: to say that an omnipotent being cannot eat because it is not the kind of thing that eats (compare: you cannot 'sleep furiously', because sleeping is not the kind of thing that can be done furiously), one is saying that its field of omnipotence is whatever is consistent with its nature. But this simply defers the difficulty again. We now need to know what its nature is to know the respects in which, within the limits of its nature, it is unlimited in power. Will this satisfy the sceptic? No, because this is already to say that the supposedly omnipotent being is only qualifiedly omnipotent – and that is a contradiction in terms.

These points are neither frivolous nor pedantic, because they show that pressure on the concept of deity quickly exposes incoherences, leaving its defenders only with the ineffability move for protecting their adherence to it. But the ineffability move cannot give us an ontological argument, which crucially depends on assertions about the nature of the deity.

Notice that these thoughts, if they cannot be answered, undermine the ontological argument even before its details are examined. But let us examine them anyway; and in a stronger form that does not require a comparative notion of perfection.

The argument's most familiar version is given by René Descartes in the fifth of his *Meditations* (1641). His version has it that the concept of a non-existent 'supremely perfect being' is a contradiction, just as it is a contradiction to deny that the interior angles of a plane triangle add up to 180 degrees. Accordingly, because we can conceive of a 'supremely perfect being', it follows from the very definition of it that it necessarily exists.

The definitive response was stated by Immanuel Kant in the 'Dialectic' of his *Critique of Pure Reason* (1787), which is the section of that famous work devoted to exploring how reason can go wrong, as happens in the ontological argument. He pointed out that 'existence' is not a property of anything, but a condition of anything's having a property. In Descartes' statement of the argument, existence is a perfection which deity cannot lack, and it is therefore a property among the other superlative properties ascribable to the deity. But, said Kant, any possessor of properties cannot have its own existence as one among those properties; it must (so to speak, already) exist in order to be a possessor of properties. You cannot say of a table, 'It is made of wood, has three legs, is round, *and* it exists,' for it might have properties different from being wooden, three-legged and round, while still being a table – a metal, four-legged, square table perhaps – but it could not be non-existent and still be a table.

The point is illustrated by noting that if one thinks Descartes's form of the argument works, a parallel version of it can be used to prove that a devil must be necessarily non-existent. It would go as follows: 'There is a being which is the least perfect of all beings; such a being which does not exist is – since existence is a perfection – less perfect than one that does; therefore the least perfect being necessarily does not exist.' Here non-existence is asserted to be a property of a being whose other properties are, presumably, evil, malevolence, impurity and so forth: but one wonders how a non-existent thing can be evil and impure, thus demonstrating that existing is a logically different category from, because a logically prior category to, any properties anything might possess.

A version of the ontological argument is offered by the American theist philosopher Alvin Plantinga, who does not claim that it proves that a god exists, but that it establishes that it is rational to think that a god exists.[9] His argument turns on a standard way of explaining the 'modal' concepts *possibility* and *necessity*. Something is said to be possible if there is at least one way a world could be – a 'possible world' – such that it exists in that world. A world is a possible world if it is either our actual world (to be actual it has at least to be possible) or is a non-actual world the concept of which is without internal contradictions. And then we say that something 'exists necessarily' if it exists in every possible world – which is merely a different way of saying: a 'necessary something' is a something that *must* exist no matter what else is the case.

Plantinga's argument is as follows. There is a possible world in which something exists that is the greatest thing there can ever be (a thing which has 'maximal greatness'). Therefore there is such a thing. And then Plantinga says this thing is god. As noted, Plantinga (wisely) does not take this to prove the existence of a god, but claims that it makes belief in a god rational.

Another approach in this style of reasoning is to say that there is a possible world in which there is a necessarily existing x; and therefore x exists. And as with the 'greatest thing' in Plantinga's version, this necessarily existing thing is identified as a god.

Neither strategy works. The second formulation turns on a technical principle in modal logic: 'If it is possible that it is necessary that p then, by a certain rule, one can infer that p is necessary.' Here is the explanation: anything which is possible exists, by definition, in at least one possible world. If it is possible that there is a necessary x, then there is at least one world in which x exists necessarily. But if x is a necessary being – if it must exist and cannot do other than exist – then it must exist in every possible world, including the actual world. Therefore if it is possible that there is a necessary x, there is actually a necessary x.

Leave aside the question what such a thing would be, and why – given that it is only by stipulation that a god is a necessary being – the necessary being in question is the God of theistic tradition, and ask: what reason is there for thinking that anything exists necessarily? That is, on what grounds is it claimed that it is possible that anything is necessary? In fact, the argument is question-begging, for by saying that there is a world in which something is necessary, by the definition of 'necessary' what is thereby being asserted is that it has to exist in every possible world. Yet with equal plausibility it can be claimed that 'there is a possible world in which nothing exists necessarily' – which means 'there is a possible world in which everything is contingent' – and if this is possible (as it surely is: our own world is such a world!) then it follows that nothing is necessary, because only if it is *not possible* for there to be a world in which nothing is necessary can there be any necessarily existing thing – for remember: such a thing would have to exist in *every* possible world.

The first version of Plantinga's argument, which starts from the premise that 'there is a possible world containing a maximally great entity' is vulnerable to the challenge that one can equally start from the premise that there is no possible world in which anything is maximally great, from which it would follow that necessarily there is no maximally great thing. Are there grounds for preferring one of these starting premises to the other one? Arguably, given the problem, discussed above, questioning whether the phrase 'maximal greatness' means anything, it is the second premise which is marginally more intelligible and therefore sensible. At the least this shows that you have to begin by accepting that there can be a 'maximally great something' for the argument to have any grip; and that of course is to argue in a circle.

It would seem that Alvin Plantinga has abandoned attempts to show by argument that it is rational to hold theistic beliefs, because he now argues that there is no need to provide such arguments, on the grounds that belief in the existence of a deity is a 'basic belief' from which one begins, not at which one ends by investigation and argument.[10] By a 'basic belief' is meant such as 'the past exists', 'other people have minds', 'one plus one is two'. So Plantinga is arguing that it is just as obvious, fundamental and unquestionable that 'God exists'.

The least of the problems with this breathtaking assertion is that the supposed basic belief that 'the past exists' – and so for the other examples given – can and have regularly been challenged by rational sceptical argument, and yet they are a good deal less contentious than the claim that gods, goddesses and other supernatural beings exist, or that at least one such exists.

The main problem is that calling a belief 'basic', so that you do not have to argue for it or provide evidence for it, is gratuitous: you can help yourself to anything you like, and of course anything follows. Choose a convenient belief, give it the most convenient content for what else you wish to believe, and then claim that it is 'basic' and therefore in no need of justification. This is too obviously unacceptable to need much comment. As Daniel Dennett said of this view of Plantinga's, this is 'Exhibit A of how religious belief can damage or hinder or disable a philosopher'.

The claim that there is a deity with supernal powers has exactly the effect of claiming that a contradiction is true: nothing can be inconsistent with the existence of such a being, and therefore nothing can test whether or not it exists. It is yet again Popper's dictum, 'What explains everything explains nothing,' which shows what is wrong with that.

In Plantinga's view, the critiques of religious belief given by the likes of Richard Dawkins and Daniel Dennett are worthless: in an interview for the *New York Times* he described Dawkins as 'dancing on the lunatic fringe' and Dennett as engaging in 'inane ridicule and burlesque' rather than argument.[11] Apart from this, by its nature, being a case of the pot calling the kettle black, it comes richly from someone who thinks we have no need to provide argument or evidence for a belief in deity. Two things that stand out in Plantinga's claims are, first, that theism is more consistent with science than atheism because a universe ruled by a deity is an orderly one, and therefore fit for the operation of natural laws; whereas a universe not ruled by a deity would be disorderly and not fit for description by science. This is a bizarre view: it seems to imply that unless the universe had a ruler it would be naughty, with galaxies and stars disobeying the laws of gravity and the rest. The point Plantinga misses, in common with all apologists who wish to insert a deity into the picture, is that if the laws of nature describe the universe successfully, then it blunts Ockham's Razor to bring in an unnecessary addition to the framework of explanation for this fact.

The second point that stands out from Plantinga's views is his claim that everyone has a *sensus divinitatis* but that in some people – Dawkins, Dennett, the writer of these words – it 'does not work properly'. The Latin phrase, literally 'a sense of the divine' but meaning 'an innate conviction that god exists', is used as a booster to the claim that belief in god is 'basic' and in no need of justification. Again, this would be a very convenient view for the theistic cause, because it applies to everyone without exception; the non-believer is told that his *sensus divinitatis* is not working properly, not that he has no such thing, and this is why he cannot accept that 'there is a god' is as basic a belief as 'one plus one equals two'.

I repeat the quotation from W. K. Clifford: 'It is wrong always, everywhere, and for anyone, to believe anything upon insufficient evidence.' It has to be said that by Clifford's lights Plantinga's approach provides an example of complete intellectual irresponsibility.

10

Causes, Wagers and Morals

The *cosmological argument*, in its various forms, infers the existence of deity from observations about the contingency of the world. It is similar to the teleological argument in being empirically based, but it differs in that, instead of focusing on the appearance of design in the world, it concentrates on the facts that the world came into existence, that it could have been different (this is what is meant by the world being 'contingent'), and that everything is governed by causation – everything is the effect or outcome of preceding conditions and circumstances that caused it.

The standard form of the cosmological argument says that because the world came into existence, it must have been created, and it must have been created for the following reasons: it is contingent, so it must be grounded on something that is *non-contingent*, which is to say, *necessary*. Everything is the effect of a preceding cause, which means that the causal chain runs backwards in time to earlier and earlier causes. Now, either there is a first uncaused or self-caused cause, or there is a regress of causes going back infinitely. But this latter supposition makes no sense, so there

must be a first cause which is itself uncaused or
self-caused.

And then the usual big jump is made from 'a first cause' or
'a necessary ground for contingent being' to a god – indeed,
to the god of traditional religion.

One immediate comment that the cosmological argument
invites is to say that it is an expression of a psychological need
to have explanations about why there is a world, how it
began, and where it is going. It is a feature of human beings
that they are eager for accounts that give explanatory closure.
The scientific mindset, which welcomes the open-endedness
of uncertainty because it is an invitation to enquiry and
discovery, is the opposite of this. Notably, a religious explanation of how the world began, why it exists, and where we
are all going to end, can be given in twenty minutes or less.
It takes years to master the rudiments of physics.

Arguments of a cosmological type are found in Plato and
Aristotle, but a clear modern statement of the argument's
basic idea is given by Leibniz in his assertion that 'nothing
can exist without a sufficient reason why it is so and not
otherwise'.[12] In the physical world revealed by empirical
observation, this principle – known as the 'principle of sufficient reason' – takes the form of a causal claim stating that
every contingently existing thing has a cause of its existence.
And then the rest of the argument falls into place: the chain
of causes cannot run back infinitely, so there has to be a first
cause, and since this first cause is itself not contingent upon
or caused by anything else, it must be non-contingent, that
is, necessary.

There are a number of obvious responses, each equally
definitive. One is to question the necessity of a non-contingent first cause. Why cannot the universe be its own reason

for existing? Science has a very good account of how the universe we occupy – whether or not it is one of many, perhaps infinitely many – has evolved from a beginning whose nature can be carefully reconstructed, to within a minuscule fraction of time after the initial singularity (the 'Big Bang'), by tracing back the evolution of physical phenomena as they now are.

The logic that underlies this did not have to wait for contemporary physics to be clear. Hume argued in his *Dialogues Concerning Natural Religion* (1779) that if you explain each individual contingent thing in the universe, you thereby explain the universe, and that it is a fallacy of logic to suppose that once you have done this you still have to explain the existence of the universe as a whole. This is cognate to what in logic is called the 'fallacy of composition', which we commit if we say that because each member of a school of whales is a whale, the school of whales is a whale – in other words, that a collection has the properties of its individual members. By reasoning in an analogous way, we see that to explain each thing in the universe does not leave the universe as a whole to be explained; the sum of individual explanations does the work already.

Hume also called into question the principle of causation that underlies the argument. Why accept *a priori* that everything has a cause, given that we can conceive of effects independently of causes? Defenders of the cosmological argument say that without strict adherence to the causal principle we cannot make the universe intelligible. But this might be because of the psychological need noted above, to reduce everything to a neat explanatory framework – the universe might in fact work in ways that do not comply with our intellectual preferences.

Kant approached the cosmological argument differently in his *Critique of Pure Reason*. He argued that it is not really an empirical argument, but a concealed version of the ontological argument, for it invokes the concept of a necessary being to serve as a ground for the contingent universe. But the concept of a necessary being is shown by discussion of the ontological argument to be empty.

Some of Kant's critics use a technical philosophical distinction to answer him. They claim that he has mistaken the idea of a *logically necessary being* with the cosmological argument's requirement for a *metaphysically necessary being*. The distinction works in rather the way that equivocation over the term 'necessary' worked in relation to Dr Pangloss's nose, as explained above. A logically necessary being is one that must exist. A metaphysically necessary being is one *that must exist in order for the universe to have a stopping-point for the regress of causes*, that is, as a ground on which contingent existence can rest. Thus, metaphysical necessity is relative, logical necessity is absolute.

But Kant can reply that this attempt to restrict attention to the 'necessary condition' sense of 'necessity' is spurious, because what is being proposed is a being that *has to exist*, whether our ground for asserting this is the definition of the being (as the ontological argument has it) or the contingency and causal dependency of the world upon such a being (as the cosmological argument asserts). Any counter to the claim that the idea of a necessary being makes sense is therefore a counter to both arguments.

Some defenders of the cosmological argument position it as a version of the 'inference to the best explanation'. This move has it that because of our ignorance about the why and how of the world, nominating a deity as both its source and the reason for its existence is 'the best available explanation'.

This is a very feeble argument; it clutches arbitrarily at something to fill the explanatory gaps in our knowledge, and has no better claim than if we just as arbitrarily invoked the existence of fairies for the same purpose. Moreover, to summon so undefined and implausible a thing as a deity to perform this role is to explain the universe in terms of something more mysterious and arbitrary than the universe itself. That takes us nowhere.

The arguments so far discussed all aim to establish the proposition 'that God exists'. They are arguments that date from the long era before natural science began to give us a far better grip on the nature of natural phenomena and their operations and sources. They are arguments spun out of semantics and armchair philosophising based on very little real knowledge of the world. They wear their inadequacies on their sleeves, and such interest as they have belongs to the history of ideas – a great archive of surpassed speculations.

A quite different tactic is to argue that it is prudent to believe that there is a deity, whether or not one can otherwise provide reasons for thinking so. In fact, this move is specifically aimed at supporting belief in a deity of the traditionally conceived type, that is, one that is interested in human beings on this planet to the point of promising rewards for obedience and worship, or punishments otherwise.

The most celebrated such argument is *Pascal's wager*.[13] Pascal said that because the existence of a deity can be neither proved nor disproved (here he was mistaken; see above) by rational argument, one has to take the different course of considering the advantages and disadvantages of believing that there is a deity. If there is a deity, the advantage of believing in its existence is huge; it is a benefit that pays off for all eternity. If there is no deity, then one has not lost much by believing in its existence anyway. Therefore, it is prudent to believe.

In contemporary theory this argument is stated in terms of 'expected utility'. Pascal's point is that no matter how small the probability that a deity exists, as long as it is non-zero the utility of believing it far outweighs the disutility of believing it; therefore it is not just prudent but rational to believe.

Some theistic critics put the interesting argument that this very pragmatic reason for believing is too cold and calculating to be the kind of belief that an interested god would want from its creatures, and this might count against the utility of believing in this way; if such a god exists but is offended by the calculating nature of the belief, the sought-for benefits will not be forthcoming. So Pascal's prudential argument is self-defeating.

Voltaire's response to Pascal's wager was characteristically acute: 'the interest I have in believing in something is not a proof that the something exists'.[14] This is of course right. But the two chief criticisms of Pascal's argument are that its starting-point does not do what is required of it, and that it is not the case that the existence of a deity cannot be disproved.

First, Pascal says that as long as the probability of a god's existence is non-zero, then the utility of believing in it outweighs the utility of disbelieving in it. Note that this is only so if, in addition, you believe that there is life after death, heaven, reward and punishment, indeed a whole raft of additional things that Pascal simply assumes accompany belief in the existence of a god. If the probability that there is a god is vanishingly small, what is the probability of the truth of all this additional matter?

Grant for a moment that Pascal's prudential calculation applies to these things too. Now consider that by parity of reasoning the same amount of sense can be made of the claim that there is a non-zero probability that fairies exist, however vanishingly small that probability is; or that the gods of Olympus exist, or even that there is green cheese beneath the surface of the moon. Admittedly the utility of believing some of these things will be very low or even negative, but there could be utility in believing some of the others: belief in fairies, for example, might yield a great deal of charm and pleasure, and it might even add explanatory value. (It used to be believed that fairies were responsible for curdling milk, and for stealing small household objects such as pins and shoelaces.) In no such case could the usefulness of believing these things by itself make it rational to believe them.

This point applies to other forms of a prudential or, slightly differently, pragmatic argument. It is sometimes claimed that theistic belief should be encouraged because it makes people behave better, or because it comforts them in time of trouble, and that it can discipline whole populations by making them believe that they are being watched always and everywhere, and that they will inevitably, no escape possible, be rewarded or punished for what they do. The utility or the prudential value of this is offered as making (the inculcation of) belief rational. This is where it is relevant to revisit the points about proof made earlier, and fully worth repeating.

It was noted that in formal systems of logic and mathematics, proof is demonstrative and conclusive. In deductive logic all inferences are actually instances of *petitio principii* because the conclusion is always contained in the premises, and deductions are merely (even though often not obviously) rearrangements of the information in the premises (consider: 'all men are mortal; Socrates is a man; therefore Socrates is mortal'). As noted earlier, there can indeed be psychological novelty in the outcome of a deduction, but never logical novelty; this latter only happens in inductive inference, where the informational content of conclusions goes beyond the informational content of their premises. For this reason inductive inferences are known as 'ampliative'.

But inductions are not proofs in the sense of formal proof. Their success or otherwise turns on how probable the premises make the conclusions, or – differently and better viewed – how rational the premises make acceptance of the conclusions. And this relates them to the non-demonstrative sense of 'proof' which is at issue here.

In non-demonstrative contexts 'proof' is to be understood in its proper meaning of 'test'. Steel and other materials are tested or 'proved' – loaded until they crack or break, heated until they warp or melt, frozen until they shatter, or whatever is appropriate – and this is the sense in which we talk of the 'proof of the pudding' or 'the exception that proves (tests) the rule'. Claims to the existence of anything are subject to proof or test in this sense. This is where Carl Sagan's 'dragon in the garage' example demonstrates its worth.

Again remember Clifford's strictures on belief. When the evidence is not merely insufficient but absent or contrary, how much more wrong to do as Doubting Thomas was criticised for not doing, and as Søren Kierkegaard encouraged: to believe nevertheless.

This point weighs particularly against those who, in similar vein to Plantinga but with less disguise in theological or philosophical clothing, claim that one can *choose* to believe because it is comforting or satisfying to do so, or because it gives hope even if one knows that it is the very slimmest of hopes. These are psychological motivations which are no doubt very common among adult believers (children, as we saw, believe because they are evolutionarily primed to be credulous, and therefore believe everything the adults in their circle insist that they believe). But Clifford's point about the ethics of belief demands that we make mature and responsible use of our cognitive capacities, and nothing that Pascal or anyone else (William James had a similar view[15]) says in the way of prudence, caution, hope against hope, or the benefits of believing even on poor grounds, can stand against that.

What of the *moral argument* for the existence of deity? We need only the briefest discussion of it. Stated at its simplest, it is that there can be no morality unless there is a deity. Put a little more fully, the argument in effect says that there can be no moral code unless it is laid down, policed, punished and rewarded by a deity. Religious apologists would prefer to state the case differently: that morality is the response of a loving creation to its loving creator. Or, alternatively put again: because god is so nice, we should be nice to each other. The existence of moral evil (the tsunamis and childhood cancers) raises questions about the love and niceness of the deity if there is one, but the positively spun versions of the moral argument do not hide the fact that it consists in saying that morality is groundless unless ordained, and its breaches sanctioned, by a deity. This view is consistent with the assumption made, in the case of Judaeo-Christian religion, that humans are 'fallen' or innately sinful beings who need salvation.

The argument that there can be no morality unless policed by a deity is refuted by the existence of good atheists. Arguably, non-theists count among themselves the *most* careful moral thinkers, because in the absence of an externally imposed morality they recognise the duty to examine their views, choices and actions, and how they should behave towards others.

Consider the thinkers of classical antiquity – Aristotle, the Stoics and others – and one will see that their examination of ethics was not premised on the belief that morals were a matter of divine command, or that they were responding to the requirements of a deity, still less that they were seeking reward in an afterlife, or the avoidance of punishment. Their example illustrates the falsity of the claim that moral principles can only come from an external agency.

Nor were these thinkers persuaded that supposed analogies between moral and natural law suggest that both require to have been laid down by a deity; nor again that the only ground for the actual or even apparent objectivity of ethical principles is that they are the product of a divine will.

Kant, this time in his *Critique of Practical Reason* (1788), demonstrated one way to underwrite the objectivity of moral law; he argued that reason identifies the categorical (unconditional) imperatives that specify our moral duties, and that this would be so whether or not a deity exists.

There is an important point implicit in this view. The fact that anyone commands us to do something is not by itself a reason why we should do it, other than prudentially (as when we are threatened with punishment for not obeying). The action in question has itself to be independently worthy of doing, or there has to be a reason other than someone's merely wishing or commanding that we do it, to serve as a genuine reason for it.

A related consideration, called the 'Euthyphro Problem' after a discussion of it in Plato's dialogue of that name, is this: is an act wrong because a god says it is, or is it forbidden by god because it is wrong? If the latter, then there is a reason independently of the will of a god that makes the act wrong. But then there is morality without god and the moral argument for the existence of god fails. If the former, then anything god commands (murder and rape, for example) would be morally good, just because he commands it; and then, as Leibniz puts it, 'In saying that things are not good by any rule of goodness, but merely by the will of God, it seems to me that one destroys, without realising it, all the love of God and all his glory. For why praise him for what he has done if he would be equally praiseworthy in doing exactly the contrary?'[16]

Behind the thought that there needs to be a god to give and enforce moral principles is the further thought that such principles require the backing of authority, for otherwise there is no answer to the moral sceptic who asks, 'Why should I be moral? Why should I not lie or kill or steal?' because there is no ultimate sanction for his failure to live morally. To thinkers of this persuasion, morality is empty unless it can be enforced.

The examples of the good atheist and the classical philosopher also rebut this view. There are many sound reasons why we should seek to live responsibly, with generosity and sympathy towards others, with care and affection for them, and with continence, sound judgement and decency in our own lives. We can see the value of these things in themselves, and from the point of the benefits they bring society and its individual members, including ourselves. A thoughtful person could decide not to be the sort of person who steals even if he would never be found out or punished, precisely because he does not want to be such a person, and because at least one person knows what he would be doing if he did such things – namely, himself; and if he has standards, he might well choose to live up to them.

In short, there is no need for an external enforcer to make us the kind of people who take such thoughts seriously; and we might all prefer to live in a world where people seek to be morally worthy because they see the point of it, not because they are being watched and will be rewarded or punished according to the degree to which they abide by the rules. In the latter sort of world one cannot tell the difference between those who are acting out of principle and those who are acting out of prudence, and perhaps wishing they could do otherwise – doing it inauthentically, as the point is sometimes put. How much better is a world for being a world of volunteers, not slaves!

II

Creationism and 'Intelligent Design'

There is no discussing religion without addressing its effect on social policy, medicine and medical research, moral questions, and its relation with science. I discuss the first three in Part II.

On the last point, there are broadly speaking three schools of thought: that science and religion are compatible because they address wholly different spheres; or they are compatible because the principles, practices and world-views of science and religion (more accurately, some religions, or some sects of some religions) are consistent with each other; or, thirdly, that one of them is right about the world, and the other one wrong. For a long time – from the fifth century of the common era (C.E.) when the church closed the Schools of Athens for teaching philosophy (which included science) right up to the seventeenth century – religion took the view that it was right and science was wrong, and anyone who disagreed might be killed (for example, Giordano Bruno) or obliged to recant under threat of death (for example, Galileo). Educated opinion now has matters the other way round: religion is wrong, science is right (more accurately, that

scientific method and ideas are increasingly giving us a better
and more practical understanding of the world and ourselves).
This is regarded as an arrogant thing for science to say, or for
anyone to say on behalf of science; perhaps a sense of fairness
has it that religion and science should each be allowed to
have a bit of being-right. This kind thought is however not
to the point: ultimately the debate is about which way of
thinking and justifying beliefs is the one that will take us
towards the truth.

Whatever else one might think about the chequered
history of the relation between religion and science, at least
one thing is clear: that they do indeed compete for the truth
about the origin of the universe, the nature of human beings,
and whether the universe manifests evidence of intelligent
design. Religion also competes with secular philosophy over
the question of the foundations of morality and whether the
existence of the universe and humanity serves a purpose set
by a supernatural agency, or whether the making of moral
meaning is the responsibility of human beings themselves.

Some of these points have already been addressed in the
preceding pages. In this chapter I look at one major example
of where religion – in the form of certain Christian sects and
Islam – directly disagrees with science. This is the matter of
'Creationism' and its most recent avatar as 'Intelligent Design
theory' ('ID theory').

Since the humiliating defeat of the literal six-day creationist lobby in the Scopes Monkey Trial of 1925 in Tennessee,
religious groups have grown increasingly sophisticated in
their efforts to promote the idea that the universe and life in
it were made by an intelligent agency, just as a carpenter
makes a table; except that whereas a carpenter has his planks
and nails to hand when he starts, the mega-carpenter did not

have any materials ready beforehand, but made them too, from nothing. Six Day Creationism, based on a literal reading of the book of Genesis in the Bible, therefore mutated (one should say – evolved) into new guises, first as 'Creation Science' and then – yet more sophisticatedly – as ID theory.

Creation Science purports to show that the geological and fossil record is explicable as the outcome of two events: a single act of creation by a god, and a subsequent worldwide flood. On this view vegetarian Tyrannosaurus Rex shared Eden with Adam and Eve, and so great was the weight of waters in the Flood that what looks like aeons of geological strata were laid down in the short span of time between the rain and the dove's return to Noah's Ark.

ID theory is a disguised version of this. It does not invoke either of the two creation myths in Genesis directly, but tries to argue on putative scientific grounds that there is irreducible complexity in nature that can only be explained as the outcome of conscious and intelligent design. Its proponents thereby construct a Trojan Horse for Creationism by arguing that their theory, as a scientific theory, should have equal time in schools with Darwinian biology.

Creationism and ID have received repeated setbacks in American courtrooms as school boards in more traditionalist states have tried to insert a religious agenda into the teaching of school science, only to be contested and consistently defeated by defenders of the US Constitution's First Amendment, which requires strict separation of state and religion.

Nevertheless the money, organisation, propaganda effort and persistence of the religious lobby is remarkable. A notable example of one of the bodies set up to promote the agenda is the Discovery Institute in Seattle, which describes itself in its promotional literature as 'a nonpartisan public policy think tank conducting research on technology, science and culture, economics and foreign affairs'. The apparent neutrality of this description is belied by the fact that its major if not sole endeavour is to promote ID theory and to get it taught in schools, at the very least alongside standard (which means, evolutionary) biology, although doubtless the eventual aim is to displace standard biology.

In 1984 Laurie R. Godfrey edited a collection of essays entitled *Scientists Confront Creationism*. In 2008 she returned, in company with Andrew J. Petto, to address the evolution in efforts just described; the earlier collection confronted Creationism, the later volume confronted both Creationism and ID.[17]

Although both books prompt one to lament the time, energy and effort that genuine scientists have to waste in combating this agenda, distracting them from real work because of the need to defend science and education from Creationism-ID's corrosive effects on both, it has to be confessed that the essays make entertaining reading. A prime example is the discussion by Victor J. Stenger of William Dembski, whose use of statistics and information theory to 'prove' that biological systems are too complex to have evolved naturally have been ID's mainstay. The idea of 'irreducible complexity' is the key to the ID case, which it maintains in the face of overwhelming observational and experimental evidence that complexity with emergent properties is a commonplace of natural processes. What appears to underlie ID theory's insistence that complex structures cannot be explained as outcomes of the accretion of simpler structures is that they do not know enough chemistry or biology to see how in fact it happens.

CREATIONISM AND 'INTELLIGENT DESIGN'   III

The really surprising thing about ID theorists is that they miss the larger point about explanation, which is that to explain something by invoking something itself unexplained is to provide no explanation at all. Exasperated parents sometimes put an end to persistent 'why?' questioning by small children with, 'Because it just is!' This is in essence the ID theorist's view about the origins of the universe and life, and about complex natural structures: any difficulty in understanding them invites from them the closure of 'God did it'. But what work does this claim actually do? The child's question presses: if the universe and life in this corner of it had to be designed by a god, what is this entity that it could do such a thing? Is it complex, and therefore – on the terms of the ID theorist's own argument – in need of a designer in its turn? If so, that designer must have been complex too, if not indeed more so, and would need another designer in its own turn – and so on ad infinitum. Since explanatory regresses with no first term explain nothing (and this applies also to the idea that the designer always existed, without a beginning), the alternative is to say that the designer designed itself. But if so, how might that work? With a snap of its antecedently non-existent fingers?

In short, the explanatory value of the idea of a designer or deity to 'explain' in its turn the universe and the complexity of life in it is null.

This prompts consideration of the real motivation behind the ID theorist's desire to persuade us that there is not just room but a need to accept the existence of a designer. Clearly, it is to open a conceptual gap into which the deity of traditional revealed religion can be inserted. The aim is to establish premises for an antecedently accepted conclusion. ID theorists know in advance the answer, and are seeking to arrange the right questions to get to it; they know what they wish to prove, and are suborning evidence which, when properly applied and understood, leads to very different conclusions. They subscribe for non-rational reasons to one of many creation myths from the infancy of mankind – the Judaeo-Christian biblical one; this applies to Islam too, which is a product of this tradition – and are looking for justifications in support of it. This is as far from science, rationality and intellectual honesty as one can get, and it is the essence of the Creationism-ID project.

The ID project addresses itself mainly to biology in opposition to evolutionary theory. Creation science addresses itself mainly to the physics of cosmogony and cosmology, on the origins and nature of the universe. They overlap when they invoke the fact that life could not exist on this planet unless the constants of nature were fine-tuned exactly as they are. But when the scientific data do not support their aims, they find ways to suggest that the parameters of nature might change over time, or differ in different circumstances. Take just one example in illustration. Creationists contest isotopic dating techniques which show that the Earth is billions of years old by suggesting that 'since the Creation one or more episodes occurred when nuclear decay rates were billions of times greater than today's rates. Possibly there were three episodes: one in the early part of the Creation week, another between the Fall and the Flood, and the third during the year of the Genesis flood' (this quotation is from a publication by a creationist group calling itself RATE – Radioisotopes and the Age of the Earth). For this suggestion to be true would require changes in fundamental constants including Planck's constant and the speed of light, which in turn changes the nature of light and many other physical and chemical properties. The universe would not exist if this were the case – or it would be a very different one. Such is the quality of thought in Creationism-ID 'science'.

The *bête noire* of the ID lobby is Charles Darwin. Their arguments are aimed at establishing that he, and the evolutionary biology that, with genetics, has grown from his work, are plain wrong. But there are more moderate religious voices that attempt a different tactic, that of saying that Darwinism is compatible with religious belief. Because concessive and compatibilist moves by religious apologists have as part of their aim the protection of religion from refutation by science, this is in its way a more insidious matter than the blunt opposition from Creationism-ID views. This is because Darwinism is not compatible with religion; the evidences of biological science are evidences against the presence of supernatural agency in the universe. This merits fuller explanation, as follows.

'Darwinism' is a term now used as a general synonym for evolutionary theory in biology. Biological evolution is a fact even though detailed questions about its mechanisms continue to be explored. The name 'Darwinism' has, familiarly, been used for a number of variants and offshoots associated with Darwin's discoveries, although his concept of descent with modification is at the core of the modern evolutionary synthesis, which among other things has added to his original insights discoveries about genes, population genetics and deeper understanding of how speciation occurs. I shall use 'Darwinism' to denote this synthesis.

As noted, I use the phrase 'religious belief' throughout this book to mean any belief in the existence and planet-Earth-focused activity of supernatural agencies, or one such agent (a 'god'). The question at issue is whether Darwinism, as just explained, is compatible with such religious belief in this focal sense.

There are many historical, anthropological and psychological reasons for the many different forms of religious belief which, now as throughout recorded history, have variously been held by different groups of people, but as noted earlier – and this is important for the present discussion – it is certain that one common feature of early religion was that it served as a form of proto-science and proto-technology, in the sense that it offered explanations of natural phenomena and a means of influencing them through ritual of various kinds. This is the feature of early belief systems that persists today in the view that the origin of the universe and life was a purposive act by a suitably equipped agency: exactly the view of the Creationist and ID theorists.

A large part of the philosophy of classical antiquity – the point at which enquiry of a recognisably scientific stamp enters the record with Thales, Anaximander, Parmenides, the atomists Democritus and Leucippus, and others – consisted in the search for non-supernaturalistic and non-fabulist accounts of the nature of things. The Greek thinkers premised their views on the recognition that Creationist accounts are projections from the human experience of agency, and that their plausibility rested on the absence, at that time, of any better explanation. This anthropomorphic projection seemed all the more plausible to those who also believed that the planet we inhabit is the chief feature of the universe, lying at its centre with all the heavenly bodies orbiting it, and that mankind is its chief ornament. For such people, the belief that the world and we in it are the work of a deity who takes a close interest in us seems entirely appropriate.

It appears not to have occurred to them that attributing the origins of the universe and life to a conscious agency merely defers the explanatory task. Definitions of deity as eternal or self-caused are arbitrary and obviously ad hoc; theology seeks to protect them from charges of meaningless-ness by describing them as 'mysteries' lying beyond human comprehension. All these moves accord with the natural psychological need of humans for everything to be explica-ble in narrative form, with beginnings (and future endings: religion offers detailed accounts of these too) to provide neatness and closure for thought.

Modern science, after a long intermission in which people could invite death if they dared think differently from what religious authorities imposed as dogma, resumed the tradition begun by the Greek philosophers of examining questions about the world on the basis of observation and reason, with-out recourse to religious explanations. But until the nineteenth century's advances in geology and biology, the question of the origin of life on Earth was an open one, even though many (from classical antiquity onwards) had hypothesised – on good observational grounds – forms of evolution, and had noticed the similarities between different species. I noted earlier that because it was social suicide to profess atheism until the later nineteenth century, most people who expressed views about matters on which religion claimed knowledge were content to call themselves 'deists', taking the minimalist view that an agency created the world and then ceased either to exist or to be interested, thereafter playing no further part. This is the residuum of the explanatory need to have something to say about beginnings. It is unlikely that many intelligent folk really believed this idea; one mark of intelligence is an ability to live with as yet unanswered questions.

Darwinism demonstrates the redundancy of the idea of a creator-designer agent in biology. More, it shows that such an idea is inconsistent with the observable facts of nature in general, as clearly as the geological evidence shows that 'Young Earth' Creationism is false. This is the key point: for if Darwinism is not compatible with religious belief as such then it is not compatible with any particular version of religious belief such as Christianity.

Religious apologists who say that their views are compatible with Darwinism accept that biological evolution occurs over great periods of time, yet say that a deity is involved in designing and sponsoring those processes. Consider a parallel. Suppose it was once believed that flowers are coloured because fairies paint them while we sleep. Once we understand the natural processes by which flowers come to be coloured, it would not merely be redundant but contradictory to claim that *in addition* to the biological process that causes floral coloration, it is also part of the explanation that they are painted (in the very same colours) by fairies. For if the biological account is correct, the fairy-tale account is false (and vice versa): one cannot hold both to be true together.

However, most religious apologists who accept that biological evolution occurs just as the Darwinian synthesis states, do not claim that it is a dual process, happening by natural and simultaneously by supernatural means. Instead their claim is that a deity planned and initiated the evolutionary processes in question, and then let it take its course; and that it is for this reason that religion and Darwinism are compatible.

But these apologists are in the same situation as a fairy-believer would be who claimed that although floral coloration is indeed the outcome of wholly biological processes, these latter occur *because fairies want them to occur* (evolution happens by wholly natural means *because a deity willed that it should*). Each of the following objections is fatal: the claim adds nothing to the biological account, requires very considerable independent motivation, and − even more fatally, if that is possible − that *any arbitrary superfluity whatever* of this kind is 'consistent' with the biological account. In other words, to claim that fairies designed the world to look and behave as if it was not designed by fairies is consistent with science − because of its meaninglessness.

As a last resort some defenders of religion might concede that Darwinism removes the need to invoke a purposeful agency to design living things or govern the changes and variations among them, but they still argue that the concept of a deity is needed for other explanatory purposes − for an example noted earlier, to explain why we must be moral, by arguing that the deity exists to enforce morality with promises of reward and threats of punishment. The fallacy here is quickly pointed out: some atheists can be highly moral; they do not need the concept of a rewarding and punishing deity, nor is a morality worth much if it only exists on the basis of promises and threats.

Again consider a parallel. Suppose that fairy-believers at last accept that floral coloration happens naturally, and begin to invoke other arguments instead to support their belief that fairies exist. Suppose they say that the concept of fairies is still required to explain why (say) people find the colours of flowers pretty − perhaps by putting fairy-spells on them. What is notable in this effort to find work for fairies to do, now that flower colouring is denied them, is the fact that the chief *raison d'être* for hypothesising their existence in the first place has gone. Thus it is with the religious who concede that the world and life do not require a creator, but find alternative employment for the concept of an agency whose original *raison d'être* was to create the world and life.

Another tack that can be taken to show the incompatibility of Darwinism and religion again concerns those concepts of 'design' and 'purposive design'. Traditional revealed religion assigns omnipotence, omniscience and benevolence to deity. The presence of natural evil in the world – the suffering it contains as a result of predation, disease and such occurrences as droughts, floods, earthquakes and volcanism – prompts even theologians, or some of them, to regard the alleged characteristics of omnipotence and benevolence as incompatible: one of the two has to give. But what most emphatically rebuts the attempt by some religious apologists to accord deity a hand in evolution – and this especially applies to Creationists and ID theorists – is the obvious fact that if organisms were purposively designed, the designer would have to have been mighty incompetent, wasteful and cruel. The biological realm universally manifests evidence of emergent naturally occurring design, the result of the mechanisms by which descent with modification works – including many imperfections, redundant organs, dead-end lines of development, new problems caused by genetic adaptations to 'solve' old problems, and the like.

A further inconsistency, therefore, obtains between religious beliefs about the existence and development of life, and the observable facts of biology: biological 'design' is manifestly not the outcome of previous planning and execution by an intelligent purposive agency, unless that agency is markedly incompetent (for example, the optic nerve making a blind spot at the centre of the retina) or markedly malevolent (for example, the prevalence of agonising diseases).

It has to be taken seriously that Darwin himself saw, in the light of his observations and discoveries, all credibility vanish from religious beliefs. Baptised an Anglican, his early religious observance was Unitarian, a rational and liberal outlook which he abandoned for more traditional Christianity while at Cambridge, where he was greatly impressed by Paley's *Evidences* and *Natural Theology*, containing the classic statement of the argument from design. Having given up the study of medicine while at Edinburgh University, Darwin contemplated becoming a clergyman.

First, though, he joined the *Beagle* as gentleman companion to the ship's captain, Robert Fitzroy, a biblical literalist who required everyone aboard his ship to attend daily worship conducted by himself. It is interesting that Darwin collected the evidence for his great discoveries, profoundly influenced by the geology he observed and which screamed aloud the vast age of the planet, while he was in the constant company of a fundamentalist who regarded every word of the Bible as literally true, down to its account of the six days of Genesis and the creation of fixed species in the Garden of Eden.

Darwin began the voyage a practising Christian, and by its end five years later was full of doubt. He had read the first volume of Charles Lyell's three-volume *Principles of Geology* (1830–3) while at sea, and later remarked that it was the basis of 'everything which I have done in science'. Lyell showed how ancient the world really is, giving Darwin the necessary aeons for biological evolution to occur. In the late 1830s Darwin wrote 'that the Old Testament was no more to be trusted than the sacred books of the Hindoos or the beliefs of any barbarian'; not long afterwards he wrote of the New Testament that 'the more we know of the fixed laws of nature, the more incredible do miracles become . . . the men of that time were ignorant and credulous to a degree almost incomprehensible to us'. Even then he hung on to a residual Christian commitment until – by his own account – 1849: he wrote 'I never gave up Christianity until I was forty years of age.'

'Christianity' meant 'religious faith' in general; when at a dinner party in Darwin's company the Duke of Argyll said that he saw the operation of purposive mind in nature, Darwin shook his head. The traditional pre-scientific beliefs of religion simply could not survive scientific insight into nature, and Darwin experienced that truth first hand.

Darwin's profound change of view – his own biography is a microcosm of the movement of increasingly educated mankind from a religious to a secular scientific understanding of the world – was the result of immersion in the scientific method. The adventure of modern science owes itself to three things: the experimental method, the development of appropriate mathematical concepts, and – in its early modern development in the sixteenth and seventeenth centuries – the adoption of a naturalistic outlook premised on liberation from religion's hegemony over permissible thought. This last claim is directly provable: 'In disputes about natural phenomena,' Galileo wrote in a letter to an admirer, 'one must not begin with the authority of scriptural passages, but with sensory experience and necessary demonstrations.' Galileo said this when it was dangerous to say it: the Copernican heliocentric view, which has the Earth orbiting the Sun, directly controverts the statement in Psalm 93:1 that 'He hath fixed the foundations of the earth for ever, that they may not be moved.' Giordano Bruno died at the stake in the Campo dei Fiori in Rome for agreeing with Copernicus instead of the psalm.

Mention of Copernicus tempts one to think that the scientific revolution can be given a precise starting date: 1543. This is the year of publication of two highly significant works: Vesalius's treatise on anatomy, correcting the errors of ancient medical authorities on the basis of Vesalius's own practical endeavours in the dissecting room, and Copernicus's *De Revolutionibus Orbium Coelestium*, establishing the superiority of a heliocentric model of the universe over the ancient Ptolemaic model with a stationary Earth at the universe's centre.

Ptolemy's geocentric universe far better suited theological orthodoxy, as the psalm shows. The Copernican view, accordingly, was heresy.

From these momentous beginnings science has cumulatively revealed more and more about our universe, from astronomy to the microstructure of matter, from the chemistry of air to the nature of living organisms. Although no single individual is indispensable to the objective and testable progress of scientific investigation, naturally enough individuals of genius figure large. But the key is the scientific method, the formulation of hypotheses and the subjection of them to public and repeatable test.

Standard sketches of science history tend to leap from the first spectacular advances of the seventeenth century (Galileo, Newton) to those of the nineteenth (Darwin). But this is to neglect the crucial if less dramatic contributions of the eighteenth century, when carbon dioxide and oxygen were identified, and water was shown to be not an element but a compound; when the first periodic table was outlined, and the first understanding of electricity attained – with the names of such individuals as Luigi Galvani and Alessandro Volta becoming attached to the phenomena they studied. This was the century in which Joseph Priestley advanced the cause of reform as well as chemistry, when Benjamin Franklin flew kites to invite lightning strikes, and when Antoine Lavoisier, investigator of the structure of air, was condemned to the scaffold in the French Revolution. Between them these men made more than just their different contributions to the political transformation of their world.

Science also has its less-sung heroes. For example: the discovery of electrons, X-rays and radioactivity – and therefore the ensuing atomic physics of the twentieth century – was made possible by a technological advance in the 1850s which at the time seemed a relatively minor matter, namely, the development of an effective vacuum tube. It was invented by a man named Heinrich Geissler, and it made possible the experiments on which those important developments turned. Geissler is obscured by the shadows cast by the giants who followed him, but very few in science would prefer to be a nobody than a Geissler.

Science has immense significance for our times, not least the biological sciences, where recent advances in under-standing and manipulating genes promise profound changes in medicine and agriculture, and perhaps in the very nature of humanity. No doubt this last thought is one of the reasons for alarm among traditionalists, who see it as 'playing god', and would like to halt these developments or even put the clock back to something more familiar and, they think, safer.

It is not just the biological sciences that trouble traditional-ists. Cosmology and astronomy since Copernicus have demoted humanity from the centre of the universe and the pinnacle of creation to a corner of a galaxy among billions of galaxies. Many of the dramatic advances in our understanding of the universe turn on improved ways of measuring the distances to stars and galaxies, and determining their composition. Speculation about the origins and nature of the universe (respectively, cosmogony and cosmology) constituted some of the earliest intellectual endeavours of mankind, unsurprising when one considers the experience of our remote ancestors, gazing up at the spectacular display of the heavens on clear nights uninterrupted by light from Earth; a display in which the luminous occupants of heaven wheeled majestically by at different rates, some configurations remaining forever the same, others changing in regular patterns, with the occasional startling novelty of a comet or a supernova giving rise to new surmises about gods leaping across the sky or being born and dying. How strange, beautiful and powerful it surely seemed: science makes it seem yet more beautiful, and far more interesting.

The point about advances in biological science reminds one why it matters that people should be encouraged to inform themselves as much as possible about the developments which are likely to affect their own and their descendants' lives, so that they can participate in decisions about how those changes are managed – or even whether they should be allowed. Public debate about these matters is too often vitiated by ignorance and the tendentious effect of religion-influenced views. These latter do not advance the cause of an intelligent assessment of what we know and how to use it; rather, they hinder that process, making matters worse.

The lack of success that Creationists and ID theorists have had in challenging the scientific consensus, and in getting their views into education, has encouraged them to try alternative channels. They cannot be faulted for persistence. In the United States the alternative strategy has been to get state legislatures to pass 'Academic Freedom' bills which would allow or even require teachers in high schools and colleges to teach 'Creation Science' and ID theory alongside or even instead of evolutionary biology and any science that is inconsistent with religious dogma.[18]

A cognate strategy has been to use the difficulty that the Creationist lobby has encountered in the refusal of courts to allow school boards to specify creation-promoting biology textbooks, and to 'embrace evolution fully' including all criticisms and difficulties that evolutionary theory meets with – among them, the criticisms advanced by Creationists!

This itself reveals the problem. There are detailed technical debates in science about the mechanisms of selection, whether it can apply to groups or populations as well as individuals, how the genetics of heritability work, and more. But the fundamental principle of descent with modification as a result of environmental pressures favouring the reproductive prospects of those best adapted to them – the basic Darwinian premise – is not in dispute in science, any more than is the law of gravity or the speed of light. Every major plank of scientific theory supports it, including DNA analysis, the fossil record, geological timescales, and biological observation and prediction. There is no scientific dispute over the fully established theory that all life on Earth evolved from a common ancestor living more than four billion years ago.

Yet it is precisely this fundamental tenet that the Creationists are trying to impugn, exactly as critics of religion seek to impugn the very basis of theistic belief rather than getting involved in internal disputes between, say, Catholic and Eastern Orthodox Christians over the word 'and' (this being the source of the Great Schism between the two communions: does the Holy Ghost 'proceed' from the Father *and* the Son, or the Father alone? One says 'and', the other not[19]).

The *Wall Street Journal* account of the Creationist lobby's legislative endeavours makes interesting reading.

> In the scientific community, while there may be debate about the details, the grand sweep of evolution is unassailable. 'There's no controversy,' said Jay Labov, a senior adviser for education and communication with the National Academy of Sciences. But Gallup polls consistently show that nearly half of American adults reject evolution. A third are upset that schools teach it, according to Gallup. Several states, including South Carolina and Pennsylvania, have passed science standards requiring students to think critically about evolution. Ms. Scott, of the science-education group, regards the academic-freedom bills as a more serious threat to evolution education because they give teachers so much latitude. 'This is basically a get-out-of-jail-free card for creationist teachers,' she said. So far, few teachers have come forward in favour of these bills. The Florida Education Association, which represents 140,000 teachers, opposes the concept.[20]

No scientists would wish students *not* to 'think critically' about anything; when South Carolina and Pennsylvania passed 'science standards' requirements that students 'think critically' about evolution, this was code for allowing Creationist criticisms of evolution to creep into formal public education.

Why are these evolution wars so bitter and perennial in the United States? Because whereas other Christian communities, such as the one in Nigeria, might have large fundamentalist and literalist wings, in the United States the members of this wing live in an advanced society where the power of science is everywhere in evidence, and so the tension between religion and science is more acutely felt. The Creationists recognise that science radically undermines religion. That is why they fight it with such vigour and resolution.

Conclusion to Part I

The case against religion is, as the foregoing shows, a cumulative and far-ranging one that casts its net wide because the phenomena, the motivations and sources, the arguments and the psychology that together go to generate and sustain religion, are themselves so diffuse and dispersed. The cumulative case against religion shows it to be a hangover from the infancy of modern humanity, persistent and enduring because of the vested interests of religious organisations, proselytisation of children, complicity of temporal powers requiring the social and moral policing that religion offers, and human psychology itself. Yet even a cursory overview of history tells us that it is one of the most destructive forces plaguing humanity. This remains true despite the positives of art, music and inspiration that religious apologists can point to as the contribution of some of their most sincere votaries. Even at the personal level where its claims to console and encourage individuals are often borne out, it is also too often a tormentor as well, plunging people into agonies of guilt over sins and fears of damnation.

Why cannot we have art and music, personal consolation and inspiration, a positive and humane outlook on life, without the ancient superstitions of our remote ancestors as their supposed source at the cost of the divisions, hatreds and torments that they bring with them? The answer is: we can. The next Part of this book shows how.

PART II

For Humanism

12

The Three Debates

In the now often acerbic debate between religion and its critics, a debate which has escalated as religion-inspired terrorism has made the critics more outspoken by far than they used to be, the arguments have gone backwards and forwards with relatively little advance because they have failed to start from clear premises. This is especially so because most participants fail to notice that not one but three separable debates are in progress, which get confused with each other and therefore confuse the participants. Each debate is important, and each has natural links to the others; but the terms of each are different, and if this is not clearly seen there will continue to be more heat than light in them.

The three separable debates are as follows. There is a theism-atheism debate, which is about metaphysics, that is, what does or does not exist. There is a secularism debate, which is about the place and volume of the religious voice in the public square. And there is a debate about the source and content of our moralities: does morality come from a transcendent source such as divine command, or does it arise from our own reflection on human realities and relationships? This is where humanism enters the picture, as a deep and powerful alternative to religious morality.

There are close connections between these three different debates, but not inevitable ones. An atheist is of course going to be a secularist and, almost certainly, a humanist. But a religious person can be a secularist, believing in the separation of religion and state; and there are some religious people who also think of themselves as humanists of a kind, though not the kind that atheist humanists understand by this term.

The first part of this book focused on the theism–atheism debate, the debate about whether one or more supernatural agencies exist in or in relation to the universe. I shall here add only one point more on this.

Theistic claims that supernatural agency exists in the universe derive from ancient traditions of belief. The word 'atheist' is a theist's term for a person who does not share such beliefs. Theists think that atheists have a belief or set of beliefs, just as theists do but in the opposite sense, about theism-related questions. This is a mistake; atheists certainly have beliefs about many things, but they are not 'theistic-subject-matter-related beliefs' in any but a single negative sense. For atheism is the absence of 'theistic-subject-matter-related' belief. Although it is true that 'absence of belief in supernatural agency' is functionally equivalent to 'belief in the absence of supernatural agency', theists concentrate on the latter formulation in order to make atheism a positive as opposed to a privative thesis with regard to theistic-subject-matter-related matters. This is what makes theists think they are in a kind of belief football match, with opposing sets of beliefs vying for our allegiance. What is happening is that the theists are rushing about the park kicking the ball, but the atheists are not playing. They are not even on the field; they are in the stands, arguing that this particular game should not be taking place at all.

The correct characterisation of the opposition between theism and atheism is therefore this: the theist has existential beliefs, metaphysical beliefs, of a certain distinctive kind; and the atheist does not share them, and therefore does not even begin to enter the domain of discourse in which these beliefs have their life and content. Rather – to use a by now familiar simile, but it exactly captures the point – atheism is to theism as not collecting stamps is to stamp-collecting. Not collecting stamps is not a hobby. It says nothing about the non-stamp-collector's other hobbies or interests. It denotes only the open-ended and negative state of not-collecting-stamps. To think of non-stamp-collectors as theists think of atheists, stamp-collectors would have to think that non-stamp-collectors have stamp interests of (so to speak) a *positively* negative kind; that they share their own obsessions and interests about stamps *but in reverse*, for example in the form of hating stamps, deliberately doing stamp-related non-stamp-collecting things, and the like.

The incoherence of the stamp-collector's attitude to the non-stamp-collector as thus described shows why 'atheism' is a misleading term, and why *a fortiori* expressions like 'militant atheist' and 'fundamentalist atheist' so miss the point. How could someone be a militant non-stamp-collector? Since atheists are equally dismissive of claims to the effect that fairies and goblins exist and have an influence on human affairs, why not call them afairyists or agoblinists instead? From the atheist's point of view, talk of goblins has an exact parity with talk of gods and goddesses.

The accusations of militancy – which at least some religious people take pride in for themselves: think of 'onward

Christian soldiers' and 'the church militant' and the like – does however apply to secularism. Some secularists are decidedly robust in their argument that religion should be kept out of government and education, as indeed the constitutions of such states as the United States and Turkey require. The militancy applies to the vigour with which the principle of secularism is asserted, not the principle itself.

The standard secularist position is this: that religions and religious attitudes (however much one disagrees with them and thinks them mistaken, retrogressive, oppressive and sometimes downright dangerous) are entitled to exist and be expressed in the public square, but with no greater privilege than any other voice in the public square. This means that religious organisations should see themselves for what they are, namely, civil society organisations of the interest-group variety, existing to put their point of view and trying to persuade others to accept it. Political parties and trade unions and other NGOs are in the business of doing this, and religious bodies are the same kind of thing as these organisations. They should therefore take their turn in the queue alongside them, and like them rely on the actual support they can muster from individuals and their donations. But they try – and for historical and institutional reasons very often succeed in this effort – to get to the front of the queue by claiming special privileges such as charitable status, state funding, traditional seats at the high table of society and state, and the 'respect due to faith' (this is a claim of very dubious respectability, since it asks us to admire views that disdain the rigorous tests of verifiability or falsifiability that we ask of claims in every other domain of enquiry). In some countries religious organisations have official state sanction for their privileging above other NGOs. This is what secularists oppose, and now that religion is reasserting itself as a problem in the world, some oppose it vigorously. Hence 'militant secularism'.

There is a true, important, though harsh-sounding point to be made about the origins of the major religions influential in today's world: that they derive ultimately from the superstitions of illiterate herdsmen living several thousands of years ago. That is a mere fact, not a rhetorical flourish. As we would expect, religious apologists say that the content of what those herdsmen thought and believed is a message from the gods, and that herdsmen were chosen as the message's recipients in preference to the learned and wise, precisely because of the virtuousness of their unlettered simplicity.

Now add together the fact of the privilege accorded religion in state and society, and the fact that the basis of the beliefs and practices of religion originated in the minds of illiterate herdsmen several thousand years ago: and you see a reason for concern about the place of religion in the public square. That is what makes some secularists militant in their opposition to the influence of religion there.

But what does this militancy involve? When the 'church militant' lived up to this title, as already noted above, it put people to death who defied it. Secularists do not aim to burn religious apologists at the stake. They use arguments. Religious apologists say they find the robustness and frankness with which secularists express their views 'offensive', and therefore complain. Secularists think there is much more to complain about in the views of too many of the religious apologists, such as, for example, that women are inferior to men and that homosexuals should be punished as criminals – the list could be a long one. It is doubtful therefore whether secularists will cease speaking out as robustly as they do merely because religious apologists feel offended. It might be said that secularists are vastly more offended by religion's negative effects on individuals and the world than the religious are for being told that their claims and assertions are spurious.

Having registered these points, we can focus on the real significance of secularism. This, to repeat, is the principle of maintaining a separation between religious interests and bodies, on the one hand, and the state, on the other hand, on the premise that religion has no greater claim than any other self-interest outlook in debates about matters of government and public policy. It should be added that an immediate consequence is that religion has no greater claim than any other viewpoint for an airing and discussion in educational programmes: and this is an important matter because of the competition between some forms of religion and, for example, science and civics education, a vexed matter as we noted in connection with Creationism and ID theory.

Defenders of religion often fail to see that a secular dispensation is actually a defence of religious organisations, in the sense that a religion-neutral public domain allows a variety of such viewpoints to exist, whereas the danger of there being a single dominating religious outlook is that others come to be marginalised or even (as history abundantly teaches) persecuted. This is happening today in the Middle East as Islamism – political Islam – rises to greater prominence; Christians in Egypt and Iraq and Jews in Morocco are suffering revived persecution. This leaves aside the fact that bitter rivalry between the Shi'ite and Sunni sects of Islam is the major reason for violent death in both populations.

Allowing a plurality of viewpoints is essential to a liberal civil society, and this means allowing different religions to co-exist, respecting the need to be peaceful and tolerant of others. A secular dispensation provides just such a setting.

There have been secular dispensations, such as the Soviet one, where religions have been actively persecuted. This is a misleading example, however, because the fact is that communism was the dominating ideology which would not brook alternatives, behaving rather as (for example) Islam does in countries where other religions are in the minority and regarded as second-rate or undesirable. This reflects the fact that religions and political totalitarianisms share a structural feature. As totalising, encompassing, monolithic ideologies claiming the one right answer and the one correct way of life, they have historically been intolerant of alterna-tive views, and have sought to quash them: this was the same, as already remarked, in Stalin's Soviet Union and Torquemada's Inquisition-devastated Spain.

As Voltaire noted, religious liberty depends on religious pluralism, and by extension the liberties of an open society depend on an even more general pluralism which is neutral with respect to any view other than the liberal view itself. But by its own nature, the liberal view is in principle tolerant and inclusive. Its only dangers are that it might inadvertently tolerate the intolerant too far; and that it allows its own beneficiaries to be lazy about protecting the liberties accorded them.

Secularism is the institutionalisation of liberalism in this sense, rendering the public domain one where any view can exist, providing it is tolerant of other views and is prepared to exist alongside them, even if it wishes to change those other views by argument and debate. That is what is meant by a

secular domain, and in this one respect it is not only consistent with but also friendly to religion.

In a truly secular world, one where religion has withered
to the relative insignificance of astrology, tarot card divination,
health-promotion based on crystals and magnets, and other
marginal superstition-involving outlooks, an ethical outlook
which can serve everyone everywhere, and can bring the
world together into a single moral community, will at last be
possible. That outlook is humanism.

13

Humanism: The Ethics of Humanity

In essence, humanism is the ethical outlook that says each individual is responsible for choosing his or her values and goals and working towards the latter in the light of the former, and is equally responsible for living considerately towards others, with a special view to establishing good relationships at the heart of life, because all good lives are premised on such. Humanism recognises the commonalities and, at the same time, wide differences that exist in human nature and capacities, and therefore respects the rights that the former tells us all must have, and the need for space and tolerance that the latter tells us each must have.

Humanism is above all about living thoughtfully and intelligently, about rising to the demand to be informed, alert and responsive, about being able to make a sound case for a choice of values and goals, and about integrity in living according to the former and determination in seeking to achieve the latter.

A succinct way of characterising the humanistic life comes from a conversation that begins Plutarch's essay, 'The Dinner of the Seven Wise Men'. Two of the sages are discussing an interesting question on their way to the dinner, as follows:

'We know what the duties are of a host at a dinner party; but what are the duties of a guest?' The other replies, 'The duty of a guest is to be a good conversationalist – that is, someone well-informed, who can articulate his views, express and explain them, make a case for them, and be prepared to change them if offered better arguments or evidence; but who is also a good listener, who hears what his interlocutors say (not what he thinks they have said), can engage with their views, discuss them, debate them, challenge them if necessary; but along with them seek clarity, understanding, and truth.' I paraphrase a little, but this was the gist. And it beautifully illustrates the humanist ideal; that the humanist is one who seeks to be informed, reflective, alert, responsive, eager for understanding and for achievement of the good: in short, to be a good guest at the dinner of life.

As the foregoing shows, in the sense now given to the word 'humanism' is a general label for ethical views about the nature of the good and well-lived life. It concerns the fundamental question – a question that everyone has to consider – of what matters in life, and its answer is premised on the view that ethics must be based on our most generous and sympathetic understanding of human nature and the human condition.

Humanism is the concern to draw the best from, and make the best of, human life in the span of a human lifetime, in the real world, and in sensible accord with the facts of humanity as these are shaped and constrained by the world. This entails that humanism rejects religious claims about the source of morality and value. As explained above, it is not the same thing as either secularism or atheism, but it has natural links to both.

The key point about humanism is that it is an attitude to ethics based on observation and the responsible use of reason, both together informing our conversation about human realities, seeking the best and most constructive way of living in accordance with them.

Although the *word* 'humanism' has a relatively short history, its main current meaning applies to the ethical tradition that began in classical Greek antiquity, older by nearly a millennium than Christianity, older by more than a millennium than Islam, much richer and deeper than either, and as alive now as it was in its origins. It is, in short, the tradition of ethical debate in philosophy, which provides the substance even of applied Christian ethics, having been borrowed by the church when, after the expected 'second coming' failed to materialise and seemed to have been postponed indefinitely, it proved necessary to import many of the ideas of the Greek ethical schools – not least from Stoicism – together with much metaphysics (chiefly in the form of Neoplatonism). The process of domiciling Greek philosophy into Christian theology was effected mainly by the Schoolmen of the late Middle Ages, chief among them Aquinas, who borrowed notably from Aristotle, whose *Nicomachean Ethics* is a classic of humanistic thought.

It was however the Renaissance that rescued humanism from its subordination to Christian theology. The Renaissance was in essence the rediscovery of classical literature and its attitudes, a rediscovery that gave birth to a broader, fresher, more open and humane spirit of enquiry than the narrow theological obsessions which had dominated the medieval mind. Renaissance humanism, also called 'literary humanism', was chiefly concerned with the study and enjoyment of history, poetry, philosophy, drama, letters – in short: the humanities.

It was then possible for educated people to enjoy the classics and the wider horizons they offered, while at the same time adhering to the conventions of church faith. This is what is meant by the 'religious humanism' of the period. An outstanding example of a humanist in this sense is Erasmus of Rotterdam. He was the Renaissance equivalent of today's international celebrity; his writings were widely read and had great influence on the culture of Europe. Their effect was to entice many away from too narrow a view of religious orthodoxy, thereby helping to create the atmosphere in which the Reformation occurred, though Erasmus himself never left the church. Because the attractions of classical literature always threatened to affect minds in this way, both the Roman Catholic and the Reformed Churches in the sixteenth century tried to suppress interest in it and to substitute more acceptable alternatives. One outstanding result was Sebastian Castellio's translation of parts of the Bible into beautiful Ciceronian Latin. This was designed as a textbook to provide schoolboys with a good model of Latin prose without harming their morals, as the works of Ovid and Virgil were thought likely to do. Both authors – not to mention Catullus, or Suetonius's account of the unsavoury examples of behaviour among the emperors – would certainly have introduced ideas into young minds that the church could not approve.

In the United States today some Unitarian and Universalist groups call themselves humanists, which to all practical purposes they are, though 'proper' humanists (so to speak) often remark that the effect of what members of those groups do is to take religion out of religion while retaining the name of religion, using 'religion' as a synonym (humanists would say, a misnomer) for 'philosophy of life' or as akin to its metaphorical use in 'football is his religion'. Either way this usage succeeds only in introducing confusion where there is no need for it, given that the basis of humanism, as described above, is that we are to answer the most fundamental of all questions, the question of how to live, by reflection on the facts of human experience in the real world, and not on the basis of religion.

One of the chief influences on Renaissance humanism was Cicero. The beauty of his prose inspired Castellio and his fellow educationists, but it was the subject-matter of his writings that inspired Erasmus and others. Erasmus said that when he read Cicero's *De Senectute* (*On Old Age*) he was moved to kiss the book, and thought that Cicero should be beatified as 'St Cicero'. The man considered to be the father of the Renaissance, Petrarch, was also an admirer of the great Roman, and yet other admirers swore that they would never write Latin in any but Cicero's way, using only the vocabulary that Cicero used.

What his Renaissance followers saw in Cicero was, precisely, his humanism – meaning this in today's sense of the word – and as with today's humanism, it was premised on a belief in individual value. Cicero held that people should be free to think for themselves, because they possess rights; but at the same time they should be conscious that their rights define their responsibilities to others. Our ethics should be premised, he said, on the fact that all humanity is a brotherhood: 'There is nothing so like anything else as we are to one another,' he wrote in *On Laws*; 'the whole foundation of the human community' consists in the bonds between people, which should reside in 'kindness, generosity, goodness and justice'. The possession of reason places on individuals a duty to develop themselves fully, and to treat others with respect and generosity. These ideas are the essence of humanism today.

These enduring connections between classical, Renaissance and contemporary humanism are striking. But the form that contemporary humanism takes is expressly secular, and owes this to the most significant period in the birth of the modern world.

Secular humanism in the form we know it now was given its first full expression in the eighteenth-century Enlightenment. Labels such as 'Enlightenment' (and 'Renaissance' and 'Reformation') are somewhat facile, collecting very complex phenomena in ways that obscure their detail, and too often making us forget that, as with everything in history, there was much opposition to the trends which we now generalise under those names. All this said, it is undeniable that the two centuries that succeeded the eighteenth century saw immense advances in science, technology, education and literacy, accountable systems of government, the rule of law and regimes of human rights; and these are the achievement of the Enlightenment. The tribulations to which humanity subjected itself during these same centuries – salient examples are the wars, the atrocities of Stalinism and Maoism, the Holocaust of European Jewry in the 1940s – are largely attributable to counter-Enlightenment efforts to resist and reverse these achievements, by reasserting or reinventing monolithic ideologies purporting to be custodians of truths to which everyone must submit. The church had been the paradigm of such a monolith, seeking – for a long time with great success – to exercise hegemony over minds and imaginations. Stalinism and Nazism likewise opposed the pluralism, individualism, freedom of thought, and the application of concepts of law and rights, that the Enlightenment had successfully opposed to the former tyrannies of church and absolute monarchy.

Thus it is that the secular humanism of today is the corollary of the maturation of humankind that the centuries of modernity, from the sixteenth century and especially the eighteenth century, have prompted and promoted.

Ideas of a distinctively humanist stamp are however not restricted to the Western tradition. Equally ancient in their roots, they are central to Confucianism and the tradition of non-theistic ethical schools of India. One interesting way to indicate the richness of humanistic thought is to nominate the authors who would figure essentially in a reading list for a study of humanism: they include Confucius, Mencius, Thucydides, Epicurus, Cicero, Seneca, Pliny the Elder and Pliny the Younger, Plutarch, Lucretius, Epictetus, Aurelius, Ibn Rushd (Averroes), Montaigne, Bruno, Spinoza, Voltaire, Merselier, Hume, Diderot, D'Holbach, Adam Smith, Gibbon, Paine, Condorcet, Bentham, Godwin, Shelley, Heine, Comte, Marx, Schopenhauer, Mill, Darwin, Huxley, Leslie Stephen, Spencer, Renan, Andrew Dickson White, Moncure Conway, Charles Bradlaugh, Robert Ingersoll, Mark Twain, Samuel Butler, W. E. H. Lecky, John Morley, Nietzsche, W. K. Clifford, G. W. Foote, Freud, Dewey, J. B. Bury, Bertrand Russell, Gilbert Murray, Chapman Cohen, G. E. Moore, Einstein, E. M. Forster, H. L. Mencken, Sir Julian Huxley, M. N. Roy, Barbara Wootton, Sydney Hook, H. J. Blackham, Jean-Paul Sartre, A. J. Ayer, Peter Medawar, Jacob Bronowski, Bernard Williams, Daniel Dennett, Christopher Hitchens, Sam Harris, Victor Stenger, Richard Dawkins – to name only a few.

Almost all these figures – and most of them explicitly – share a commitment to a fundamental premise: that the human good is for human responsibility to discern and enact, without reliance upon, or invocation of, any of the many religions which claim a transcendental source of authority, and posthumous rewards or punishments for obeying or failing to obey it.

As a broad ethical outlook, humanism involves no sectarian divisions or strife, no supernaturalism, no taboos, no food and dress codes, no restrictive sexual morality other than what is implicit in the demand to treat others with respect, consideration and kindness. It is a strikingly positive outlook, and one that would go far, if universally adopted, to solve the problems of today's world because it insists on the central importance of good relations between individuals in respect of their humanity, not in respect of what identities might overlay their humanity – the political, ethnic, religious, cultural, gender identities that so often trump the possibility of a straightforward human-to-human friendship that would cross all boundaries. This is the obverse of the coin whose reverse is the principle that individuals should be autonomous, free to think for themselves, and fully possessed of rights as well responsibilities.

It can be seen from the foregoing that humanism is an outlook based on two allied general premises, which between them allow a good deal of leeway to what follows from them. This accommodates the obvious fact that humanists might engage in political and moral debate with each other about practicalities, perhaps differing about the route to ends that they otherwise agree are desirable. Obviously enough, all reflective people are entitled to do so, and the result is debate and discussion about how to achieve the best. So, humanists can be humanists but disagree on aspects of politics, and the complexity of applied moral problems can suggest different humanist strategies for dealing with them. But such differences do not affect humanism's two fundamental premises.

The first premise is that there are no supernatural agencies in the universe, and the second, connected, premise is that our ethics must be drawn from, and responsive to, the nature and circumstances of human experience. It therefore starts from the fact that human beings exist in an entirely natural universe, governed by natural laws, and that the human good is shaped accordingly. As just acknowledged, there can be much debate about what the human good can and should be, and that debate encompasses many aspects of politics, philosophy, social thought and law. But such debates are distinctively humanist only if they reject efforts to decide or resolve them by invoking supernatural powers as the authority which dictates what the human good should be.

Religion, by contrast, is expressly premised on the idea of an external, supernatural source of moral authority. In the standard case it is held that the agencies which possess this authority are personally interested in having humankind conform itself to their purposes; and the religions in which they figure further teach that petition and sacrifice can influence those purposes. All the faiths employ prayer, ritual and sacrifice to achieve this, the last ranging from the repetition of religious formulae to slitting the throats of sacrificial victims. Unless an outlook premises the existence and interest of one or more supernatural beings, and claims that the utmost importance attaches to believing in them and responding to their requirements, it cannot be called a religion.

This, to repeat, is why neither Buddhism in its original Theravada form, nor Confucianism, are religions; they are philosophies, and atheistic ones in the literal sense of this term. The same applies to Stoicism, as we saw; for half a millennium before Constantine, Stoicism was the outlook of most educated people in the Hellenic and Roman world. Their principle of reason (the *logos*) as the ordering principle of the world is a principle of rational structure, of rightness and fittingness in the natural order, to which ethical endeavour – so they argued – should conform itself. The Stoics did not worship or petition the *logos*, and did not think of it as a person or as conscious or purposive. It would have to have been regarded as these things if it was to qualify as a god, and for interest in it to count as a religion.

The theatrical aspects of religion – church services, the Mass, hymn singing, weddings, funerals, baptisms – answer a need many feel for taking special notice of significant moments of passage in life. Communal celebrations of these moments are important to those taking part, and serve as a bonding experience for the group. Organised humanism, recognising the importance of marking life-passages like these, offers non-religious versions of some of these observances, marriages and funerals chief among them. But it is a failure of imagination not to see that when people go to concerts or exhibitions, enjoy country walks, gardening, gathering with friends round a dinner table, reading, creating something, learning, working at something absorbing and worthwhile – whatever refreshes and lifts the heart, and brings fulfilment – they are in different ways satisfying the needs for creativity, recreation, community and friendship which are vital to lives well lived.

In the past, when unlettered peasants gathered together from their farms every Sabbath, they thereby combined communality, theatre and (if they were in a church with murals) art. It was practically the only resource they had for these things, and the art – as church art – was almost exclusively didactic and sometimes coercive, driving home important lessons from the teachings of the sect they belonged to. The social resources for meeting the human needs for companionship and art have greatly expanded since, and people can now choose from a variety of ways, suited to their temperaments and talents, for satisfying what once had only that limited and always propagandistic form.

Humanism is a philosophical outlook, but in itself is a minimalist one, deliberately so because a key requirement of it is that individuals should think for themselves about what they are and how they should live. Standardly, a philosophy is a fully fleshed-out affair, consisting in a detailed view of the world, of humanity in it, of the relationship between human beings and the world, and of human beings with each other. All the great philosophies have a metaphysics that underwrites the ethics they urge. But humanism requires no commitment to teachings beyond its two fundamental premises, and it imposes no obligations on people other than to think for themselves. Because it does not consist in a body of doctrines and prescriptions, backed by sanctions for not believing in the former and not obeying the latter, it is as far from being like a religion as anything could be.

This last point needs making because religious apologists try to turn the tables on people who hold a naturalistic and humanistic outlook by offering them a *tu quoque* argument, charging them with 'faith' in science or 'faith' in reason. But they seem to forget that faith is at its most distinctive when it is opposed to facts and reason; the point of the Doubting Thomas story in the New Testament is that it is more blessed to believe without evidence than with it, and the philosopher Søren Kierkegaard was one of many who embraced the very absurdity of what faith requires as a leap of faith. Such views are what prompted Mark Twain, in his usual barbed way, to offer the definition of faith quoted earlier – faith is 'believing what you know ain't so' – and this is probably close to the truth in many cases; but a more accurate rendering would be 'faith is believing what all the evidence and the most careful use of reason tells you ain't so'.

Faith is not needed in order to 'believe in' science and the use of reason. Science is always open to challenge and refutation, faith is not. Reason must be rigorously tested by its own lights, faith rejoices in sometimes being unreasonable. In its adherence to scientific canons of observation and reason humanism is, once again, as far from sharing the characteristics of a 'faith' outlook or religion as it can be.

All this said, it remains that each humanist, starting from the shared premises that frame an overall humanistic attitude to life and the world, must work out what that means given his or her own talents for creating a life truly worth living, in both the following respects: that it feels good to live it, and that it is beneficial in its impact on others. In the pages to follow, one version of a humanist ethics is sketched. It is not intended as prescriptive, or as closing debate on any of the topics it touches; it is illustrative of a humanist endeavour which proceeds from its chooser's own efforts to fulfil the one humanist obligation: to think.

14

Humanism and the Good Life

It is well, always, to begin with clarifications, especially with so large a concept as 'the good life'. What is meant by the phrase? The answer is obvious enough if couched in general terms: it is the well-lived, meaningful, fulfilled life. But the point is to give content to each of those general ideas. We want a genuine grasp of what meaning and fulfilment are, and how we can create them in the practicalities of living in the way real lives are actually lived. And that means in the midst of difficulties, demands, setbacks, accidents, good luck and bad luck, the demands that other people make, our own limitations, and all within the constraining circumstances of a society whose parameters impose a straitjacket on much of what we can do. Given that so much of what happens in life is the result of external circumstances and other people's choices, is it really possible to make something truly good of one's life by autonomous effort? On a sober estimation of the likelihoods, it would seem that we have more chance of doing this, the less ambitious we are regarding what a 'good life' might be.

But to think like this is unnecessarily pessimistic. One might begin by mulling over the ideas that thinkers have come up with regarding the nature of the good and the kinds of lives that would express it. The point is not to take dictation from those thinkers, to read and then obey: rather, it is to read, discuss, and then take the best of their insights for one's own use, and to make the resulting combination of ideas one's own.

There is a rich resource in the literature, philosophy and history of the world for this. One has only to be an attentive and reflective reader, and to take every opportunity to discuss the ideas thus encountered with others.[21] Too many people still think that studying ethical ideas – for this is what the process is: ethics is the enquiry into the nature of the best kind of life – means finding the set that best suits them, and then agreeing with them. But no one these days would consistently subscribe to the ideas of just one ethical outlook, given that the Enlightenment has both taught and urged us to see that our duty is not to submit to the teachings of a system, but to learn from the best such teachings for our own individual use. That is what is meant by living autonomously – taking responsibility, thinking things through.

When people submit to systems, they are handing over to them (to those who devised them) the right to do their thinking and choosing for them. Given that almost all the major systems are religions, which moreover originated in a remote past to which most of their teachings apply, they can only be adapted to contemporary conditions by much reinterpretation and temporising, and alas – as noted more than once – by straightforward hypocrisy. An ethical outlook should be such that it is something people can live by honestly, authentically, without having to perform contortions to make it relevant or livable.

*   *   *

Although it is not the intention here to examine the great traditions of ethics in detail, but to draw on them for thinking about a humanistic conception of the good life, it is useful to have some of the salient ideas in mind.

Human beings have doubtless always given thought to how they should behave towards one another, but the earliest genuinely philosophical discussion we know of it took place in Greece in the classical period, and in origin is associated principally with Socrates, his disciple Plato, and Plato's pupil Aristotle. Socrates is recorded as trying to encourage his fellows to think seriously about how they should live. As a young man he had attended lectures and discussions on cosmogony, cosmology and physics, which were the major interests of his forebears in the philosophical tradition; but because science was then in an inconclusive and largely (not wholly) unexperimental form, it bothered him that his fellow citizens were poring over these questions while being indifferent to what he saw as far more important, namely, their moral well-being.

Plato describes Socrates as urging people to think harder about the virtues of courage, continence, justice and the rest, given that what they thought they knew about them was so often wrong. As Plato increasingly developed his own ethical theory he put it in a metaphysical form, advancing the idea that there is an eternal Idea of the Good, which is the chief of all the perfect Ideas, and which is what all action and desire aspires towards. A good life, on this view, is one that most fully accords with a vision of the ultimate good. In practical terms that meant a life of inner harmony between the different aspects of the soul, which combines appetite and intelligence in a relationship that could be unstable and troublesome unless disciplined by philosophy.

Aristotle was a far more pragmatic thinker, and in fact identified pragmatism itself – in the form of 'practical wisdom' – as the instrument that would help people achieve the good in life. He saw it as the instrument that would help people to navigate a middle path between extremes, these latter being vices while the middle path between them is virtue. For example: generosity is the middle way between meanness and profligacy; courage is the middle way between cowardice and rashness. It is sometimes hard for people to work out what the middle way might be in a given situation, in which case he or she should imitate a person who can. Anyone can attain practical wisdom, Aristotle said, making a habit of it by practising it.

Aristotle identified virtue as the exercise of practical wisdom, *phronesis*, because the possession of reason is humanity's defining feature, which makes living in accordance with it the essence of goodness.

Critics of Aristotle's ethics are not very kind to it. They describe his doctrine of the middle path as middle-aged, middle class and middlebrow. It has to be admitted that this is to some extent reinforced by Aristotle's own picture of the virtuous person as a self-satisfied individual with a stately walk. Such an individual is a *megalopsychos*, a rather forbidding term in Greek but in Latin it is *magna anima,* 'great soul', from which we get the word 'magnanimous'. As this suggests, what Aristotle thought of as a good person is very much what in English is meant by a 'gentleman', not in its social-class meaning but as descriptive of a person who is considerate, upright, honest and kind. This yields a rather different portrait of the ethical individual from the 'middle-aged middlebrow' of Aristotle's critics.

Aristotle set out his ethical views in a book now entitled *The Nicomachean Ethics*, so called because it was edited by his son Nicomachus from lecture notes he left behind. It has a beautiful chapter on friendship, which Aristotle thought was the highest and finest of human relationships. This chapter has remained very influential through all discussions of friendship into modern times. He described a friend as 'another self', whose interests are identical with one's own interests. Although that is a warm idea, it is not wholly persuasive: for surely a really good friend would recognise and accept the differences between himself and his friend, differences which would still allow them their shared interest and affection; and this would allow his friend the space to be himself. For this to be possible there has to be generosity, tolerance and understanding – the truest marks of friendship.

The unsettled state of the Hellenic period in the centuries after Aristotle prompted much discussion about how people could achieve inner security and peace of mind – what in Greek was called *ataraxia*. If outward life is uncertain and sometimes dangerous, the ethical life has to be an internal one, in one's own thoughts and feelings, which can be brought more under one's own control.

By far the noblest of the ethical outlooks to pursue this line was Stoicism, the philosophy of life of educated people for over half a millennium before Christianity became the official outlook of the Roman world. Stoicism's main doctrine was that one should cultivate two capacities: 'indifference', and self-control. They used the term 'indifference' in the strict sense of this term to mean neutrality, detachment, as in not taking sides on a question, or being disengaged from a quarrel.

Indifference was to be cultivated towards what one cannot alter or influence in the vicissitudes of life, towards things that one cannot control: earthquakes, disease, old age. In effect it meant having courage in the face of these things.

And self-command was to be cultivated in respect of all those things over which one does have control – one's fears, desires, appetites, hopes.

By cultivating and combining these two capacities, the Stoics said, one will be able to live courageously and serenely, which means: with dignity. Our contemporary concept of a stoic comes directly from this conception of a person who, despite tumults and troubles, can face them with equanimity. ('Equanimity': an equal – balanced – mind.)

The two great exponents of late ethical Stoicism were an emperor, Marcus Aurelius, and a Greek slave in Rome, Epictetus. Aurelius's *Meditations* are a classic, and Epictetus's *Encheiridion* to this day repays study. The view of life they expressed has remained influential in Western culture, although not explicitly recognised for what it is, both because of how it shaped educated sentiment in the literature of the Roman Empire and the thoughts of those who later read and learned from it, and because its principal tenets were adapted into Christian thinking once this religion came to need a richer ethics than the New Testament provided, with its thin teaching of 'give away all you have, make no plans for the morrow, turn your back on your family if they disagree with you in either of these respects, do not marry' – the ethics of people who thought they lived in the last weeks or months of history, but which after several centuries had come to be too austere for common sense.

Another ancient school that taught a way to *ataraxia* was Epicureanism. It was founded by Epicurus, who advised everyone to 'pursue pleasure and avoid pain' – although his idea of pleasure and pain make this surprising doctrine not what it seems. His view was that the conventional pleasures associated with food, drink and sex contain the seeds of pain within them, and are therefore to be avoided, and true pleasures preferred to these: learning, reading, discussing, being continent in all appetites. 'Epicureanism' has since come to mean the pursuit of the very opposite of these frugal and enduring pleasures.

Both the Epicureans and the Stoics saw involvement in the world's affairs as a duty for the responsibly minded citizen. A third philosophical movement, contemporary with them, emphatically disagreed. This was Cynicism, the school of Diogenes of Sinope, who advocated dropping out of society and living an individual self-contained life as close to nature as possible. In line with his principles Diogenes went about naked, masturbated in public, and scorned all other conventions too.

From the fifth century C.E. – that is, from the time that Christianity became the dominant outlook of Europe – until the seventeenth century, there was scarcely any debate about the foundations of ethics because it was taken for granted that all questions about how to live had been settled by the church. The church's authority was final, because it was the custodian and purveyor of God's authority, and God's word – which was not just the Bible but also the evolving teaching of the church itself – was not to be gainsaid.

In the eighteenth century, however, debate about the foundations and principles of ethics was able to resume following the liberation of thought made possible by the Reformation and the scientific revolutions of the preceding two centuries. This was not least because philosophers had again allowed themselves to acknowledge an important truth that Plato had already recognised in his dialogue *Euthyphro*, that the statement 'God is good' is not a tautology, and that therefore the question of the nature and basis of goodness is a matter that has to be discussed independently of theology.

To reprise the *Euthyphro* point, given its importance: is something good because the gods say it is, or do the gods say it is good because it is good independently of them? Only the most zealous of souls could say that if the gods decreed that murder and rape are good, this would make them good. Accordingly the reason why they are bad is not a matter of what any gods like or say, but because there is an independent reason for their being bad. And because that is so, the question of the basis of moral value needs to be discussed on its own terms.

Thus prompted to revisit the foundational questions in ethics, eighteenth-century thinkers – chiefly including David Hume, Francis Hutcheson, Bishop Butler, the Earl of Shaftesbury, Bernard Mandeville and Immanuel Kant – between them shaped the outlines of a debate that has continued since. Two major trends emerged from their work. One is consequentialism, which in essence says that the target of moral evaluation is the outcomes of actions. The other is deontology, which consists in the claim that the target of moral evaluation is the intrinsic moral nature of acts, actors and situations, independently of consequences.

In the following centuries the consequentialist theory known as 'utilitarianism' become highly influential, taking an increasing variety of forms as it was subjected to increasingly intensive debate, a debate that continues even now. From the beginning utilitarianism recommended itself as a highly practical theory, one that could be applied by servants of the Crown ruling far-flung corners of Empire. This was because its basic idea is that an act is good if it produces more good (or happiness, or 'utility') over bad (or unhappiness, or 'disutility').

As philosophy increasingly became a salaried job in universities, a development mainly of the last century and a half, discussion of ethics has ceased to be about how to live and instead has become 'meta-ethical', that is, a scholarly investigation of the words and concepts used in moral debate. It focuses on theories and on methods of 'practical reasoning', not on how to cope with grief, or to face adversity or old age, with courage and a quiet mind. But the world is impatient of too much pedantry, so, driven by real needs to confront problems of life, relationships, responsibilities and death, there has risen a whole new area of discussion outside the universities called 'applied ethics', which includes medical ethics, environmental ethics, business ethics, discussion of 'just war theory', and other major practical concerns of life and society.

The irony is, of course, that ethics always used to be 'applied' – that is, about real questions of real life – and the drift of academic debate into abstractions has meant that thinking about what should be done in difficult real-life cases has required the long-standing tradition of ethics to reinvent itself with a new name. Not that it has taken long for academic philosophy to pounce on these revived practical debates in order to haul them into the dehydrated air of the seminar room, there to pursue the irrelevances of abstraction all over again.

It has been pertinently remarked that ethics is not a subject for philosophy alone, but needs the contributions of psychologists, anthropologists, historians, novelists, dramatists and all other kinds of artists.[22] Since the fundamental subject of ethics is what kinds of lives are best, all the materials that their insights and perspectives can offer are necessary to the task – not merely desirable, note, but necessary. If one thinks about this point for a moment, one sees that it implies something deeply interesting: that one of the goods of the quest to understand what the good life should be, is the quest itself. That is a very humanistic point.

There is no suggestion in any of the foregoing that the way to make a good life is to adopt and adhere to someone else's idea of a good life: on the contrary. This is the point of insisting that people must think for themselves. Bertrand Russell's witticism that 'most people would rather die than think and most people do' is intended to focus attention on a too common human propensity, namely, the desire for other people to do the hard yards of working out what is right and wrong, and of finding out what to think and do as a result. That is one of the reasons why religion has survived into the modern world: it tells people what to think and do, gratifying their reluctance to make the effort, or to take the risk, of achieving self-understanding and on that basis choosing a course that would be a fulfilling expression of their individual talents for living well. In wanting a quick answer to 'what should I do, how should I live?' people grab a one-size-fits-all model from a shelf in the ideas supermarket, and leave it at that.

In the humanist view, that is not acceptable; it is an abandonment of responsibility, which at the same time means a loss of opportunity. The Enlightenment lesson is that there are many kinds of worthwhile aspirations for human life – indeed, given that each individual has his or her own set of talents and capacities, there might be as many different possible good lives as there are people to live them. It is a false view purveyed by monolithic ideologies – the ideologies that say there is one great truth and one right way to live, and everyone must conform, be the same, do the same, obey, submit – that there is only one kind of good life and that it is the same for all.

It follows that ethical discussion cannot be about prescribing to individuals, but must instead be an exploration of the general characteristics that the diversity of good lives tend to display, together with the general principles suggested by morally relevant facts about human experience. Consideration of these matters enters the picture when people are challenged to justify their moral choices. A life cannot be thought good which is harmful in its impact on others, or which results in a perversion of the possibilities and capacities of the person living it. A choice of life has to be able to stand up to scrutiny, a fact that rules out irresponsible, destructive, wasteful lives as good.

So – bearing in mind that by 'good lives' we mean lives worth living, fruitful and flourishing lives, lives that have a positive impact on others – we might try to identify a number of characteristics that such lives are likely to display.

One is that good lives seem meaningful or purposeful to the people living them. Another is that they are lives lived in relationships, having at their core real intimacy – love, or friendship – with one or more others. A third is that they are lives of activity – of doing, making or learning. A fourth is that they are consistently marked by honesty and authenticity. A fifth is that they manifest autonomy, that is, the acceptance of responsibility for the choices that shape the course of life. A sixth is that the felt quality of the life from an aesthetic point of view is positive; that is, the experience of living it feels rich or satisfying to the person living it.

The seventh and last is integrity, in the sense of the integration of all the others into a whole which constitutes the individual's own chosen project for the good.

Each of these characteristics merits comment in its own right. I take them in turn.

When people talk about 'the meaning of life' without intending this phrase to be a caricature of what philosophy is about, they are making an incorrect assumption which has already been identified in the foregoing: that there is one thing which is 'the meaning' of life, and by implication, the same meaning for everyone. This notion must be rejected outright. If asked, 'What is the meaning of life?' the correct answer is: 'What you make it' – specifically, what you make it for yourself, on the basis of thought followed by responsible choices that will survive challenge by others if they are sceptical about what you choose.

This shows that there is indeed real content to talk of 'meaning' in life. Meaning is the set of values and their associated goals that give a life its shape and direction. To talk of direction is to suggest a journey, or a process, a movement from choices towards their realisation through endeavour; and in various significant ways meaning is a function of that journeying.

Another way of looking at this is to see each person as the author of a narrative, one which constitutes over time his or her personal biography. Not everyone likes this metaphor because it implies the narrative's end before the narrative has reached its end, as if the story were about someone already dead.[23] Such critics urge us to accept that chance can play a part in life, which we must embrace because of the fresh opportunities it opens. This point is of course right, but to think that having a plan is to refuse in advance to take advantage of chance happenings or new opportunities if they offer themselves, is a mistake. To have goals is not to blind oneself to life's unexpectedness and what that implies. But on the other hand to be without goals is to drift, leaving one's direction in life at the mercy of other people's choices, as if one were a canoe being tossed about on the ocean by big ships steaming by. To have goals, and to be travelling towards their realisation, is to be travelling under one's own steam – but still able to change course if chance or opportunity invite.

What, though, are the kinds of goals that good lives characteristically aim at? This question does not herald an attempt at being prescriptive, given that the point is for everyone to be individually self-prescriptive about these vital matters. But it helps to have some indication of how one might frame this question so that it identifies an answer in each individual case. That help lies to hand in a compelling essay by Albert Camus, *The Myth of Sisyphus* (1942). In it he makes a surprising suggestion that does the trick: he says that the most important philosophical question we can each ask ourselves is, 'Do I or do I not wish to commit suicide?' If we say, 'No I do not,' as most of us would, it is because we have reasons for living, or at the very least real hope that we can find such reasons. Then the next question is: what are the reasons I personally have for saying 'No' to that question? The answer contains the meaning of my life.

This nails the point. Of course, though people will choose their own unique sets of reasons for finding life meaningful, it would not be surprising if they overlapped with those of others. Loving someone, having children to look after, wanting to achieve success in a competitive field, are among the common themes everyone would recognise. But it might be a lost opportunity if the reasons were entirely conventional. One of Oscar Wilde's much-quoted remarks is that everyone's map of the world should have a Utopia on it. It is said, in the same vein, that all good things began as dreams or ideals. Most things, good or bad, never become anything else; perhaps this indicates that whatever set of reasons we have for saying 'No' to Camus's question, it would be good to have something distinctive in it. This will be something that the individual cares about, and not because they are part of the conventional values that are in favour at his time.

It always sounds reductive to talk of 'conventional' values as if these, just because they are conventional – which means inherited, derived from the traditions and practices of a community – are *ipso facto* bad. They certainly can be; they can be oppressive and retrograde, a dead hand on progress, stifling and numbing. Social progress is typically the result of liberation from them. But some conventional values might consist in wisdom distilled and matured out of the collective experience of the tribe, and therefore worth thinking about, even in cases where they require adaptation to new circumstances.

No one is without a set of values, even if only those they rebel against. Most such values are vaguely defined and only intermittently lived up to. They are the residue of upbringing, school life, the cacophony of media debates over the latest moral panic or scandal, and the traces of religious instruction and sentiment. The first thing anyone must do, in thinking about why he answers Camus's question with 'No', is to take these values out into the light and examine them, rigorously and honestly. Without doubt, several of them would go straight into the bin. What they would each have to show, when appraised in the light of experience and adult reason, is whether a good case remains for adhering to them. What the person examining himself in this way would have to show, for his part, is the maturity and courage to give up what does not survive scrutiny, and adopt what does. That can be a painful process, especially when it involves giving up childhood religious sentiments and acknowledging that some parts of what one thought and believed were merely prejudices, or that they were unformed because first acquired in childhood, or unfair to others, as with the racist and sexist attitudes that likewise tend to be leftovers of childhood learning from intolerant adults in the vicinity.

The other characteristics of good lives are not additional to, but each in its way is contributory to, the meaningfulness characteristic just discussed.

It is natural to comment straight away on the fact that at the heart of good lives there are, invariably, good relationships. This is a function of the obvious fact that humans are essentially social beings. It is not only that most of a person's deepest satisfactions, security and validation come from close relationships, but that his individual character is shaped by them, especially those that dominate his formative years. This has both positive and negative implications. On the negative side, it is a regrettable fact, but one which has long sustained the profession of clinical psychology in its various manifestations, that relationships are too often the source of problems, given that they can result in the infinitely possible child being turned into the narrowly and sometimes problematically constrained adult.

When relationships are toxic, and warp rather than develop character, they are of course worse than no relationship at all. Most such relationships tend to be involuntary ones, the ones imposed on people by accidents of birth and history. In contrast, good relationships tend to be chosen ones, entered into on the basis of mutual recognition and shared interests. Put schematically, one might say that each party to a chosen and positive relationship is a fuller person for it, while each party to a toxic relationship is diminished by it.

Of course, some of our involuntary relationships – those with parents and siblings – can be the most rewarding in our lives, and even if they are not uniformly so they are sure to be among the most significant. The tie of kinship has an importance whose roots are biological rather than social, and that makes a big, though complicated, difference. But whether relationships are chosen or involuntary, the mere fact of their existence is a prompt for serious thought about the responsibilities they involve.

Good relationships make better people: that is a truism. The point is worth remembering when things go awry with this aspect of a good life project. Broken relationships, ill temper, arguments, infidelities and lies, anger, the acidification of love into hate, are at least in part any agent's own doing, however much others might have contributed to the failure. In a way it is easier to face life's external vicissitudes, the bad things that happen outside one's control. With regard to them the necessity is for courage and endurance, neither of them easy, but not always impossible. What is needed in confronting one's own part in the collapse of a relationship is quite similar. It takes honesty in addition, something that facing external challenges does not require. But it takes courage to be honest too, so maybe the Stoic injunction to live with courage applies all round.

It is useful to remember the classical Greeks' attitude to moral failure: in their view it is like taking aim at a target, and missing; it is a bad shot; what you must do is aim again, and do better. In other moral regimes failure is a blemish, a stain that remains, culpable and in need of grace or forgiveness from an outside source. In the classical view, the remedy and improvement is as much the individual's responsibility as the mistake was in the first place.

Now consider endeavour. What would a life of complete ease be like, without demands or obligations? It is an interesting speculation. A beach holiday comes closest, so there might be hints there. Consider such a thing in the extreme. How long can one lie on a beach all day, and on a bed all night, doing nothing else, nothing marked by a purpose of some kind – even reading a book? It takes little imagination to see how irksome that would become, and quickly too. No doubt there are experts at lazing who bear the burden of aimlessness and inactivity by being able to switch off mentally, or by smoking a soothing weed of some sort, but that is not the normal human response, which is far more likely to be boredom, irritation and restlessness.

The fact that these last three states arise so readily from inactivity is a good sign. They indicate why human beings do things, make things, explore, socialise, create, mend, build, decorate, tell stories, enjoy stories – read them, go to the cinema to see them enacted – namely, we are animals who thrive when engaged, and suffer from idleness. The engagement does not have to be any more taxing than reading, knitting or gardening, though for some it has to take the form of climbing Everest or going to the moon. And there are plenty of worthwhile and creative activities in between.

There are many motivations for going to the moon, ranging from increasing our understanding of the universe to the
sheer pleasure of succeeding at a difficult task. One of John
F. Kennedy's speech-writers penned some superb lines on
this theme for the President to say at Rice Stadium on 12
September 1962. That was the occasion on which Kennedy
announced the Apollo moon program, whose aim was to put
a man on the moon by the end of the 1960s. 'We choose to
go to the moon in this decade, and do the other things,' said
Kennedy, 'not because they are easy, but because they are
hard, because that goal will serve to organise and measure the
best of our energies and skills.' That is an admirable sentiment, not least for being one that is assumed to so much of
what human beings do and have always done anyway, namely,
striven for big goals – some of them horrible, it is true, but
many of them wonderful; and the civilisations of the world
are the result.

There is an allied thought. A central plank of the scientific
method is its open invitation to others to test, probe and
question the work that any scientist or group of scientists
does. The generalised version of this is the invitation to
submit oneself – one's ideas and proposals, one's efforts – to
challenge by and disagreement from others. Many people are
afraid to venture for fear of criticism or ridicule if they fail,
which means that lots of opportunities are lost that might
otherwise have proved worthwhile. But it is through failure
and criticism that one has one's best chance of learning the
best lessons. It is a commonplace to say this, but much more
common is the refusal of so many people to accept its truth
and to act accordingly.

This thought naturally introduces the ideas of truth and
authenticity, two fine-sounding but really indispensable

characteristics of good lives. Part of the reason for the usual response to mentions of them, which is a cynical raising of an eyebrow, is that they are so rarely achieved. But like most things that are valuable, the endeavour to achieve them confers a kind of nobility in its own right, providing that one is not using the claim that one is making the endeavour, but failing, as a fig-leaf for not really making the endeavour. As this implies, the effort to achieve authenticity has to be an authentic one.

The idea of a truthful life is not merely that of an honest life, lived without deception and falsehood in its portrayal of self to others, and without self-deception – an equally common failing – but one which embodies the etymology of 'true', which is 'straight' – as when we say an arrow flies true. What that involves is directness, emotional honesty, a refusal to escape into pieties, nonsense or comforting illusions, but above all an ability to 'see things steadily and see them whole' – this phrase being Matthew Arnold's description of the capacity that distinguished the ancient Athenians.

All this is vastly easier said than done, and it is a rare person who does not delude himself, or find it easier to misrepresent himself in various ways to others, or to make use of untruths as a social lubricant – as when one tells small 'white lies' to spare others' feelings or smooth over awkwardnesses. There is a good justification for judicious deception of this latter sort; it helps society to function by ameliorating relationships and preventing breaches and quarrels. In this respect one might agree with the Church of Scotland's charming dictum that 'it is a sin to tell an untimely truth'.

But as regards oneself, there is something repugnant about 'living a lie', trying to appear what one is not, misleading others, bearing the strain of imposture even in small things.

This happens far more often than is realised; it might even be the very stuff of many marriages, not in the sense of the infidelity of the partners but in the compromises, pretences and bald untruths that help to hold the relationship together. The key here is to ask oneself if one can make a sound case to anyone (one's own conscience, perhaps) who challenges one to explain and defend how one is living.

Some might think that a completely honest world would be a more boring one. Perhaps that is so. But the attrition of little untruths and prevarications in one's dealings with others and one's attitude to oneself will at some point do harm, and make one feel soiled.

The concept of truth in living can be described as authenticity, hence the point of putting the two together. The notions relate to the angle at which one stands to the world: *straight on*, if true; *obliquely*, if made up of a tessellation of little evasions; *not at all*, if patched out of lies.

To live inauthentically is to be enslaved, at least in part, to the falsity of the person one thus is. To have an answer to the challenges that might be put to one's choices and style of life is part of what it is to be free. The other part is autonomy, being one's own lawmaker at the core of one's moral being ('autonomy' translates as 'self-law'). Autonomy is the responsibility, ultimate and fundamental, for one's choices and the consequences one sought or accepted in making them. Many consequences are of course unpredictable, so it is hard to blame people for harms they did not intend when making their choices. But in their core meanings, and in their central importance to life, the linked ideas of autonomy and responsibility are clear.

This assumes that there is an answer to the profoundly difficult metaphysical question about freedom of the will. Is there is such a thing as genuine moral agency, or does every-thing – including human action – occur as the necessitated outcome of causal chains of events? The answer assumed by ethical debate is that free will exists. Without that assump-tion the entire edifice of moral discourse collapses. Of course it accepts that upbringing, the constraints imposed by soci-ety, and the finite nature of any individual's physical and mental powers, jointly make people contingently unfree in obvious ways. But the key assumption is that people are not metaphysically unfree – that is the essential point for moral theory.

That is a debate for another time and place. It is a very important debate not least because neuroscience is leading many to conclude that free will is an illusion. In the religion debate it is the religious apologists who most acutely need to defend the concept of free will for theological reasons. I think there are good grounds for defending the concept of free will on non-religious grounds: but again, that is a debate for another time. Here the premise of talking about good lives is that we are morally free to choose, and therefore we have the responsibility to choose wisely.

Most inhabitants of classical Athens were very unfree; only adult male citizens were enfranchised. But the reason why, despite this, Athens is regarded as the starting-point in the story of liberty is that the enfranchised were most of the time able to debate, enquire, challenge and criticise without having to defer to religious or temporal authorities for fear of reprisal.[24] Immanuel Kant had this in mind when defining 'Enlightenment', not as an achieved state of affairs but as a developing process which simultaneously urges and permits greater independence of thought. His essay 'Answering the Question: What is Enlightenment?' (1784) is a key text:

Enlightenment is man's emergence from his self-imposed immaturity. Immaturity is the inability to use one's understanding without guidance from another. This immaturity is self-imposed when its cause lies not in lack of understanding, but in lack of resolve and courage to use it without guidance from another. *Sapere Aude!* [dare to know] – 'Have courage to use your own understanding!' – that is the motto of enlightenment . . . Nothing is required for enlightenment except freedom; and the freedom in question is the least harmful of all, namely, the freedom to use reason publicly in all matters. But on all sides I hear: 'Do not argue!' The officer says, 'Do not argue, drill!' The tax man says, 'Do not argue, pay!' The pastor says, 'Do not argue, believe!'

The message is clarion clear: to think for oneself is essential to the good life because what flows from doing so is one's own. If others do the thinking for one, or if orthodoxies or traditions do it, one's life is not one's own. The good and well-lived life is not a servitude, but a service to one's own chosen values. So the train of thought goes: freedom is what makes it possible to create meaning in one's life, and the creation of meaning in one's life is the good life itself.

The two remaining characteristics of good lives are that they feel good to the people living them, and that they manifest integrity in the sense that all their parts fit together into a coherent whole.

The phrase 'feels good to live' might be slightly misleading; a more accurate way of putting the point, but one that sounds a good deal more precious, is to talk of the felt quality of experience, and indeed of beauty. It would be difficult to persuade anyone that a life is as good as it could be if it is monotonously grey and boring, without ornament or charm, without any of the colour, variety or amenity of the kinds that speak either to the senses or to the intelligence or – best of all – to both; and provide refreshment thereby.

In those parts of the world whose people are beset by poverty and struggle, there is little opportunity for attention to the grace notes of life. But it is remarkable how soon human creativity turns to making ornament and decoration, either of objects or of their own faces and bodies, when respite from the business of finding sustenance and shelter is over. Little else could as well show the importance to human experience than this feature of it. Art is not always about beauty, or even mainly about it, but often expresses or celebrates it. The beauties of nature are unfailingly attractive to us, and we seek them avidly. Between them, art and nature provide what is necessary and central for the setting of our experience if it is to be positive. We have all experienced how much the quality of our days is affected by their setting; these are reminders of that fact, because people forget it, and allow their settings to become habitual and monotonous, summoning the same response from within.[25]

It might seem surprising at first to be told that one of the important things about beauty is that it exercises our capacity to be emotionally moved. Sad stories, tender scenes, grief, love, laughter, do the same; and when they do it, they enhance our membership of the moral community, in making us better at understanding others and expressing ourselves. There are different ways the thought might be expressed: one could talk of education of the sensibilities, or of a sentimental education, or refinement of our psychological perceptiveness and responsiveness; but the point is the same throughout.

It would be pointless to talk about ensuring the mutual integrity of these positive characteristics were it not the case that contemporary lives are so often disjointed and fragmented, pulled in many directions simultaneously, lived in separate compartments, dizzied by the tumult of competing demands. Unity of purpose and therefore of the person himself or herself is just what is missing. It is a simple enough point that the different elements of what makes life good have to be consistent with each other, harmonious and mutually supporting; and that when they are, the result is one of balance. This should ring a bell. Plato repeatedly insists, in the *Republic* and the *Phaedrus* and elsewhere, that individual good consists in harmony between the different elements of the soul; and the later notion of *ataraxia* or inner peace is a descendant of that view. It is not that one wishes always to live in peace in that sense – too like the expert idler on his beach – but one wants there to be a place within that is always balanced and at peace. Finding it or making it is a criterion of achieving the good life.

The foregoing is one humanist thinker's response to the question: what alternative might a non-religious person offer concerning questions of ethics if religion were disposed of? It is only part of the answer, because the application of it to specific moral concerns about life, death, war, love, sex and politics still needs to be demonstrated. I indicate some of the relevant considerations on these matters in the next chapter. But the point worth making here is this: what would it add, to any of the above, to say that in addition to these considerations there is a deity or there are deities? What work would such a notion do, in adding or changing anything about good, meaningful, satisfying, creative, relationship-based lives of the kind described in the foregoing terms? These considerations arise from the resources of human experience and reflection alone, and they are completely persuasive. It can legitimately be hoped that anyone who reflects on them will agree, for that would mark the most significant fact about them: that between them they are the shared perspective of the majority among the most educated and reflective minds in the history of thought.

15

Putting the World to Rights

Humanists would of course acknowledge that there can be moral concerns about adultery, drugs, tax dodging and teenage crime, the topics that seem to take up most of the oxygen of moral debate. But they are going to insist that there are even more serious moral problems in our world, and they include violations of human rights, war and civil war, genocide, the arms trade, poverty, inequality and injustice, the continuance of slavery under other disguises, and the bitter religious antipathies that scar the face of humanity with conflict. These problems involve horrors and sufferings that no human being should experience, let alone the children and other innocents caught up in them.

Set against these major problems, the parochial and reactionary concerns over sex and drugs, hostility to gays, misguided campaigns about the teaching of biological evolution in schools, and other matters, can appear trivial. These questions preoccupy debate in rich, safe parts of the world, while atrocity and real hardship blight the lives of millions elsewhere.

It cannot be denied that some of the rich world's concerns are significant; gay rights, stem-cell research, abortion, and the large questions for humanity implied by the revolution in genetic science, are all matters that require discussion. So too do the environmental problems caused by the insatiable hunger for economic growth everywhere, in the developed and developing world alike. Failure to grapple with these latter problems threatens to make it pointless to grapple with the others, since if we do not overcome them we will not be here to enjoy the results of sorting those others out.

The claim that the greatest moral problems in our world are human rights violations, war, injustice and poverty hardly needs justification. What is unjustifiable is the way the problems continue, even indeed grow, because the self-interest of the parties who might be able to resolve or reduce them trumps everything. With very few exceptions, private individuals are in no position to make a difference to these problems. It is nations and their governments that have to do it, but they are all hamstrung by the short-termism and localism of the democratic process. It is not the fault of that process so much as the poor quality of candidates and electorates, who vote their own personal interest before almost all other considerations; so politicians are nailed to the petty hamster wheel of the electoral cycle. The whole world is hostage to squalid local compromises.

There have been fitful efforts in the course of the last hundred years to build international institutions that would be above these local and parochial concerns. The League of Nations after the First World War and the United Nations after the Second World War were in their different ways attempts to provide supranational mechanisms to promote and maintain peace around the world. The League was an abject failure, and the UN is alas not far behind. Impotent because of the divisions among its members and enfeebled by its lack of everything necessary to the chance of success – funds, personnel, enforceable legal authority and even moral authority – the good that the UN can attempt to do is limited. But that is not to say it does no good at all: for one thing, it keeps alive certain ideals, among which that of universal human rights is central.

One of the United Nations' first acts after the Second World War was to respond explicitly to the atrocities that had been perpetrated during it. It did so by committing itself to a great ideal: that of pronouncing every individual in the world a possessor of a set of basic and inalienable rights, and of getting every state to commit to protecting those rights.

The process began straight away. The UN Charter, adopted in 1945, affirmed 'faith in fundamental human rights, in the dignity and worth of the person, and in the equal rights of men and women and of nations large and small'. There followed the setting up of Eleanor Roosevelt's committee which drafted the Universal Declaration of Human Rights, accepted by all the member states unanimously in 1948.

In light of subsequent events, consisting of violations of rights by almost every state, and persistent and major violations by some egregious states, it is easy to regard these endeavours as futile. Having them on paper, making an issue of them, allowing NGOs to submit comments at meetings of the Human Rights Council in Geneva, may make little practical difference to what happens in dark cellars in delinquent countries, but it is vastly better than total silence and indifference. And one day it might start having an effect – or more of an effect, for it would be wrong to say that it does no good at all.

When the Universal Declaration was adopted it was welcomed most enthusiastically by 'Third World' countries, as they were once called, particularly those subjected to colonial rule. Symmetrically, there was some wariness in capital cities of the major powers, who suspected that a rod had been fashioned for their backs. Since then it is the developed countries that complain most about human rights violations in the developing countries, and as Muslim majority countries have grown more assertive so they are seeking to resile from the Declaration, wishing to assert their own Islamic version of rights in which (for example) women have fewer and lesser rights than men. More orthodox Muslims are not alone among religious groupings in finding the idea of universal rights a nuisance with respect to how they would most like to arrange their affairs, and they find a strong champion in China, which does not like the idea of universality either.[26]

The Universal Declaration is a brave, bold, generous document. It premises the claim that 'all members of the human family' enjoy 'inherent dignity and equal and inalienable rights' and that the best hopes for achieving freedom, justice and peace for everyone depends upon accepting this principle. Disregard for inherent rights led to the Second World War's atrocities, in response to which mankind must renew its hopes for 'a world in which human beings shall enjoy freedom of speech and belief and freedom from fear and want'. Because aspirations of this importance merit the protection of law, the UN's Declaration describes what such law should encompass. The main provisions are that everyone is born free and equal in rights; that these rights include life, liberty and security, freedom from slavery and cruel punishment, recognition before the law and protection by it, freedom of movement, freedom to express views, to participate in the government of the state, to have an education, to own property, to practise a religion, to have time for leisure, to make choices in personal life and to enjoy peace. Correlatively, the Declaration recognises that everyone has duties to others and to the community, observing which makes it possible for others to enjoy the same rights also.

These ideas seem commonplace to people in the developed world now; they are taken for granted. But for the majority of people in the world they are still merely aspirations and ideals, not realities. For victims of human rights violations they must seem either precious hopes or bad jokes. It is their experience that tells us what human rights should be – what the minimum is for people to have a chance of flourishing, what prevents people from having that chance – so although in the comfort of seminar rooms on peaceful campuses there can be scepticism about the very idea of human rights, in dark cellars and harsh prisons they – or at least the hope of them – are far from an abstraction.

But there is indeed a place for philosophical exploration of the ideas involved. Take the right to life, for example. Obviously enough, it cannot be regarded as a right to mere existence, but must imply a right to life of a certain quality and meaning. A number of important considerations follow from this. One might seem surprising at first; that the right to life entails a right to die. Even more specifically, it implies a right to die in a manner and at a time of one's own choosing, and with the help of medical technology, if necessary, to make it an easeful death. This follows because dying happens in the course of life, even though it is the very end of life, and a right to life of a certain minimum quality entails that, like anything that happens in lived experience, dying should not be unpleasant and difficult if there are reasonable means of making it otherwise.

This shows that the rights which humanity has claimed for itself have rich and interesting meanings, which need to be explored in all their implications as part of a philosophical framework for application to real experience.

A major reason for talking about human rights is that they offer humankind its best chance of a genuinely global ethics to which almost anyone can subscribe, from almost any tradition, creed or ethnicity. Technically speaking, all the world's people already agree that the International Bill of Human Rights is such an ethics, because they are all represented at the UN and are supposed to be signed up for its principles in virtue of that membership. Alas, this is only so 'technically speaking', and certain major groups – as noted, some of the Muslim states, and the Chinese – keep trying to redraft the human rights provisions in weaker forms to give themselves let-outs. There was a distinguished Chinese scholar on Mrs Roosevelt's committee when the UN Declaration of Human Rights was drafted; today China claims that the idea of human rights is a Western imposition on the rest of the world, implying that human rights are not universal and that different traditions, such as China's own, are entitled to apply their own different standards.

As this shows, there is still a battle to be won here. It is a battle that intensely interests humanists (the International Humanist and Ethical Union is one of the most responsible and persistent of the NGOs at the UN Human Rights Council in Geneva[27]) because the concept of rights is so paradigmatically humanistic: when the instruments of the international Human Rights Bill were being forged, there was no claim that their terms and principles were drawn from anything other than human experience, nor that their observance would get anyone into heaven. No, the claim was then, and is now, only that their observance would make this world a vastly better place.

16

Shared Humanity, Human Diversity

By now it is clear that a humanist is someone who starts from the premise that morality is a matter for discussion and decision in a society, not a divine imposition from beyond the stars. That immediately requires three comments in clarification.

First, a theme throughout the foregoing is that a humanist is responsible for his or her own ethics, and must be able to choose a life whose principles and activities can stand up to challenge. But I have just written that 'morality is a matter for discussion in a society'. Is there an inconsistency here? Only to those who think that ethics and morals are the same thing. They are not, and the distinction is important.

Ethics is about ethos, about the kind of person one is, about the manner and character of one's life and activity. A central part of one's ethos concerns morality, that is, the obligations and duties, the constraints and parameters that apply in one's relationships with others. But although one's ethics will shape one's moral behaviour, it is a much larger matter than morality. An example clarifies: it is an ethical matter what colour you paint the front door of your house, but it is not a moral matter unless the colour is so offensive that it upsets others, yet despite knowing this you do not care.

It is of such importance to understand the relationship between ethics and morality that it helps to note that the latter, as now understood, is a concept principally of modern times – since the eighteenth century – whereas ethics, as the far more inclusive notion, retains the significance of its classical roots.[28] As the concept is now understood, morality applies just to certain aspects of life, almost exclusively to interpersonal relationships; here is where we find strictures on telling lies, being unkind, malicious gossip, marital infidelity. No one thinks that what we eat or wear is a moral matter, until vegetarianism and opposition to wearing furs shows that it might be: here ethical considerations are applied to apparently neutral matters, thus bringing out their moral significance. Likewise, ethics can challenge conventional morality sharply.

The thinkers of classical antiquity saw all of life as the subject of ethics. Ethical quality applies to the whole person, and both one's own flourishing and the impact of one's choices and behaviour on others flow from one's character. For this reason one has to think about how one should live – for as Socrates said, 'The unconsidered life is not worth living.'

Ethics, therefore, as a far broader matter than the moral considerations it includes within it, is about the achievement of intelligent human well-being and well-doing. Ethical reflection concerns what sort of people we should be. This has implications for questions about what sort of society we should build – so that the best we can be ethically as individuals can have the best communal environment in which to flourish. Ethics and politics, as Aristotle saw, are continuous.

Understanding the distinction between ethics and morality is important because it helps us to understand both. Morality is about what is permissible and forbidden in particular realms of behaviour; ethics is about one's character. Because of this we can see that the groundwork of ethics is not rules, codes and sanctions, as is generally the case in morality, but a cultivation of character, with the aim of living a good life – which means: good to live, good in its impact on others. It might be utopian to think so, but in a community of people concerned to be ethical the likelihood is surely that the society will be a good one.

In fine, one's ethics is one's own responsibility; morality is the responsibility of a social conversation, a discussion, even a negotiation, which ethical individuals must engage in.

This leads to the second point. It will be claimed that it implies relativism to describe morality as a matter for social discussion and negotiation. If morality is the product of temporally and culturally parochial debate, then different societies will come up with different moralities, perhaps radically different, so that what is accepted in one is rejected in another, and there will be no objective standards, and consequently no common standard of adjudication between moral outlooks.

It is both true and inevitable that there will be differences in customs and moral emphases between societies, but as the comments above about human rights – and in particular the universality claimed for them – immediately entail, relativism is not what follows from those harmless facts. For there are objective facts about human needs and interests that constrain any possible morality. Very few people like to be cold, hungry, afraid, lonely, threatened, in danger, in physical pain, subjected to psychological suffering, deprived of basic physical and psychological amenities, and the like. We know, just in virtue of being human, what the least is that we require in these respects. And as these basic interests are satisfied, so we know what the next layers of human needs and interests are, and in the systems of law, morality and rights that we construct to address them, conceive of them as entitlements which entail obligations on others to respect them: fairness in all things, equality of consideration by the state, access to education and health care.

Throughout there are facts that identify the limits of what our response to others can be: which is to say that morality is an objective matter, and however different the mores and emphases between cultures and periods of history appear, there are common themes throughout.

Yet as this also implies – and this is the third comment – there is latitude in the discussion about morality about how the underlying principles are best served or applied. This is where debate enters, and negotiation. Such debate is entirely possible between humanists, who can vary among themselves in the degree to which they take liberal or conservative views about some questions – drug legalisation, say – and who may have different political outlooks on economic affairs, public service provision, the voting system, and more, while still very much being humanists.

For of course there is much more than questions of rights that makes for full human flourishing: all the arts and sciences show what we have found not just attractive but necessary for the fullest expression of human experience. This switches attention from the commonalities of human interests to their diversity: the higher-order respects in which people are individuals with their own talents and interests demands that we accept and permit a parallel diversity in the ways that people can achieve the good in their very different lives. One of the common things about people, in short, is their uniqueness.

Given this, the following comments on matters of moral debate constitute one view of them from a humanist perspective – one humanist's view – and do not express an agreed party line. But since the humanist principle is that we should start our moral reasoning from our best, most generous, most sympathetic view of human affairs, I would be surprised to find fellow humanists disagreeing very greatly, or about much.

17

The Ethical and the Moral

Among the standard and familiar *moral* cruces in most societies are such matters as marriage (who can marry, and whom?), divorce, sexual behaviour, abortion, euthanasia, and the use and abuse of drugs. It will doubtless come as a surprise to many people that what are conventionally regarded as moral challenges in these respects take on a quite different appearance when seen from an *ethical* perspective. For example, a moralist might think that divorce is a bad thing, or at very least should not be made too easy. From the ethical perspective the idea of people having a chance to find new and better relationships, when an existing one has failed and become psychologically toxic, looks like an important good. The moralist is rightly concerned about the harm done by divorce, for example to children, and the possibility that a domestic project might be saved if people were encouraged to give the relationship a chance to recover itself. From the ethical perspective the chance of trying again to build a good and satisfying life has to be done responsibly, to minimise the harm that such a major disruption causes. But the possibility of a fresh chance is of great significance, and it is a kind of cruelty to deny it to people – as the Roman Catholic Church tries to do with its blanket proscription of divorce.

Most people can be sensible, constructive and generous in thinking about moral matters, at least at times. We find ourselves being our best in these respects when a friend or family member is in trouble and needs advice. The rigid moralist, the person incapable of nuanced thought about difficult problems, might reach for a principle that someone else came up with – usually, a couple of thousand years ago in a prescriptive religious tradition – and apply it as it stands.

But when we think things through in a generous frame of mind we are more often than not able to make the two apparently competing factors just discussed – shared humanity and human diversity – work together in providing a solution. The shared basis of the human condition gives us the objective parameters for moral thought. The opposite fact of human diversity and difference gives us our motivation to think carefully and with an eye to nuance about how we engage with others. George Bernard Shaw was right in saying that we should not apply the Golden Rule – 'do to others as you would have them do to you' – because others might not share one's own interests and tastes, and one might not understand theirs: how can one be sure of achieving real insight into others' needs and desires merely on the basis of knowing one's own? How can one make what conduces to one's own good the benchmark and standard for the good of others?

The point about the objective parameters of morality arises from our having a good general understanding of the minimum conditions for human flourishing, while the second point reminds us that we always have much to learn about all the other things that can promote such flourishing on an individual basis.

In philosophical terminology, the objective parameters are the necessary conditions for human flourishing. Respecting the diversity of human tastes and interests relates to the many sufficient conditions for human flourishing.

Two points immediately follow from these considerations. The first is that if we know that others lack the necessary conditions for human flourishing, we have an obligation to play our part in remedying that situation. To ignore the call on our humanity in these circumstances is wrong. If a person is selfish enough to think that people must all take care only of themselves, even if their dire circumstances are the outcome of injustices of which they are the helpless victims, then even on the most minimal prudential grounds he should do something to help, because such problems might and probably will eventually become a problem for him too – in the way of crime, revolution, conflict or the breakdown of the social order.

The second point is that, when we understand that there is great variety among human needs and interests, we must accept and tolerate it, and be open-minded. We might otherwise make bad mistakes, and act in a prejudiced and ignorant way, to the detriment of others. This does not mean that we abandon standards: on analogy with the remark that one should not be so open-minded that one's brains fall out, we must not be so lax in thinking about morality that we resign ourselves to an anything-goes outlook. In this respect the way we judge can be guided by what we want for ourselves in the way of others' attitudes. We each want to live our own lives on the basis of our own choices, and not be over-constrained by others in doing so. We wish others to respect the space we need to carry out our projects, even when they do not understand what those projects mean to us. Because we require this for ourselves, we must extend the same consideration to others.

As noted, the point about tolerance is premised on the plain fact that we cannot always expect to have insight into interests that are widely different from our own; but that this is not an unqualified or irrevocable lax attitude. There are acts – murder, rape, torture, oppression and injustice – which are not to be tolerated anywhere at any time. This reminds us of a vital principle: that our freedom to choose and act must not result in harm to others, or prevent them from pursuing their aims under the same constraint.

The great sin, as this implies, is harming others.[29] The simplicity of the point should not mask its profundity. For it is rich in implications about the positive duties it implies towards others: for one example, if one knows another is in need, and one could help but chooses not to, is that not harming him? Only moral casuists of the slipperiest kind would say No.

There is a so far unmentioned background to all the foregoing. It is that in no human community are resources and sympathies in unlimited supply. As a result, competition between individuals and groups arise and in some (too many) cases lead to conflict. That is why laws, customs and moralities are necessary; in their respective ways they help to ease or at least manage relationships, especially when conflicts occur as with almost everything else in human affairs. How much better things work out if the way people behave comes from reflective and generous commitments to promoting the good in all things.

The principal subject matter of morality is, overwhelmingly, human relationships. As an aside, though, it should be noted that there are good arguments for including the animal and more generally the natural world in the sphere of moral concern. One source of this thought is an important distinction that is almost always overlooked both in informal and in philosophical discussions of morality. This is the distinction between moral agents and moral patients.

A moral agent is something that can choose, act, consider the consequences of both choices and actions, be held responsible for them, and be praised or blamed accordingly. The typical moral agent is a human being who has attained the age of reason, but it happens that corporate bodies are moral agents too – companies, governments, institutions – and they can be held accountable in the same way, and praised or blamed accordingly, for their moral behaviour.

A moral patient is something that is worthy of moral regard in virtue of its ability to be affected by what moral agents do. Moral agents are also moral patients, because the activity of other moral agents can affect them. A chicken is not a moral agent, but it is a moral patient; it can suffer in that it can experience pain and fear, and it can take pleasure in strutting about and pecking the ground without nearby threats; and therefore it is worthy of moral regard – of being treated in a way that is accordant with and respectful of these facts about it.

The natural environment other than the animals that inhabit it is also, arguably, a moral patient, because it has value in itself and can be harmed or benefited by the activity of moral agents. But if there are sceptics on this point we can take the alternative tack of reminding them that the natural environment at very least has instrumental value, given its importance to future generations of human beings; so we must look after it now in the interests of those future generations, whom we are thereby rightly treating as moral patients (even though they are not yet moral agents).

Efforts have been made to persuade us to count the animal world and indeed the whole of nature as objects of moral concern – as moral patients – quite rightly in my view. The indifference that meets this proposal has encouraged some (notably Peter Singer) to try starting with the more modest project of including the other great apes in the circle of moral concern along with we human apes. This would stop the slaughter – for then it would be murder – of chimpanzees for bush meat, their use in medical experiments, the destruction of their homelands which we would now regard as belonging in the fullest legal sense to them, and so forth.

I shall not pursue these points further here. I note them in order to point out that humanism is not just about humans in the sense of believing that the only worthwhile topics of moral and ethical debate are human beings and their societies. Humanism is about behaving like the best of civilised, thoughtful, responsible, considerate moral agents. We talk about being humane towards animals; that is, acting with the consideration and kindness that arise from conscious interest in their welfare. You would expect a humanist to be humane – a humane-ist you might say – in all things, including attitudes to nature and its non-human inhabitants.

All that said, it remains that the principal subject matter of morality is, overwhelmingly, human relationships. On the face of it, human relationships can take a dozen different basic forms: the parent–child relationship; the relationship between siblings; friendship; the lover relationship; marriage; work relationships with colleagues; professional relationships; casual ones; the various levels of neighbourliness; relationships with others in a group of some kind, such as a community, nation, tribe or football supporters' club; the non-relationship of indifference as when strangers pass on the street; and finally, enmity in any of its forms.

Almost all of these relationships have their inner complexity – there is hierarchy in many of them: a boss at work, an older respected member of the supporters' club, a dominant partner in marriage – and sometimes they have ill effects on the parties to them, though it is virtually impossible (for all but Robinson Crusoe, and even he had Man Friday eventually) for anyone to do without at least some subset of them. In the general run of things most relationships are enjoyed or endured because of the positive benefits they bring. Complications arise when exploitation and abuse enter them: some examples are slavery, mistreatment of children, injustice in access to social goods and possibilities in a society whose social and political structures favour one group rather than others.

18

A Humanist on Love, Sex and Drugs

If there is one thing that no human can do without, it is love. Babies and small children cannot flourish, perhaps not even survive, without it. Very few people – and these few would be highly unusual ones – do not wish to both give and receive love as one of the central facts of their lives. The love that they give and receive need not be and in most cases in fact is not the heady variety of film romance, although this looms large on the horizon of human interest; the calmer and deeper varieties of love prove in the end to be the more necessary, and the more enduring, for all those fortunate to achieve them.

To judge by the attention it receives in literature, song and cinema, romantic love has to be one of the most dramatic and important things in life. Yet conventional morality seems to require that apart from a few experiments in early adulthood, its reality should only be experienced once, with one person, and lifelong bonding should be the appropriate outcome. Anyone who claims to fall in love frequently is thought irresponsible, and with some justification: for it is such a transforming, time-consuming, exhausting, ecstatic, painful business that it takes a long time to recover from it – in some cases, whole lifetimes.

And yet one of the oddest things about falling in love is that it is not always a good way to get to know someone, for Stendhal's excellent reason that we cloak the beloved in layers of crystal, and see a vision rather than a person for the whole period of our entrancement. So: this important, universal but individually rare, intrinsically delusional state fascinates us, yet we scarcely understand it.

Some think that romantic love was invented by medieval troubadours, but it is difficult to deny that it is a universal phenomenon, given the frequency of its occurrence even in ancient literatures, and the fact that the Greeks thought it a curse when inflicted by the arrows of Cupid. If it were true that romantic love was invented by troubadours, it would be a 'socially constructed' phenomenon, and some indeed argue this. Others – and they are surely right – see it as one of the four great upheavals which define the human condition, along with birth, having children and dying.

The obsessive character of love cannot be understood without reference to sex, to which I turn below. But it is necessary to remark straight away on history's ambivalent attitudes to female sexuality, casting woman as asexual saint or as lustful devil, as virgin or whore, Madonna or Magdalene – and the other stereotypes which confuse and misdirect our thinking on these matters.

Perhaps unluckily for more trenchant feminist views, science seems to suggest that in the competition between nature and nurture, the former has an insistent and irreducible role in determining sexual behaviour and gender characteristics. This does not have to imply strict determinism: as rational beings people can adjust biology in the direction of justice, as we do when controlling our aggression and selfishness.

But sexual passion and romantic love are not very often amenable to calm rationality, and moralists have typically regarded this as a problem requiring control, a bit like an infestation of pests. But they are not problems, they are facts; it is society that turns them into problems by trying to manage, constrain and deny them, by trying to re-route, prohibit, channel and manipulate them. It is to the dead hand of oppressive institutions such as religions that one must look for an explanation of why love can be a problem: which, generally speaking, it only is when rationed and starved. Then it becomes destructive, prompting the moralisers, in their wisdom, to ration and starve it more. Thereby hangs many a long tale – which novels, poems, songs and films tell us over and over again to our inexhaustible fascination.

All this said, it must also be acknowledged that most of what is believed by young people to be romantic love is really infatuation. To say this is not to belittle infatuation; it is what renews the species, it is the solder that first fuses people together, and it allows sexual inexperience to go largely unnoticed or at least forgiven. It is the preliminary and preparatory preface to love, the romantic and youthful illusion of it, and it is this on which, accurately speaking, the poetry and cinema of the world is drunk. But it is not really, or not yet, love proper; and it is a far cry from love as it is experienced in life's more mature reaches.

Looking at love from the perspective of time is instructive. Infatuation can grow into love given time and a dose of life's realities, which romance by definition lacks. But first it has to shed its blindness – another of infatuation's defining characteristics – and its egocentricity. This is the egocentricity of hunger, the need to consume and possess the other's presence, and thereby to satisfy one's own appetite. Mature love is different. It comes when one clearly sees the other in his or her individuality, and can therefore acknowledge it; only with such distance does true closeness come. Romantic infatuation tries to negate otherness, to achieve a merging or identification as if the Hermaphroditic myth, in which lovers are sundered halves of the same being, were true. Love proper is an open-eyed recognition of separateness – but of separateness connected. That is the beauty of it; it lies in the connection, mutual and willed, that two individuals choose to make.

Such recognition and mutuality is often the gift of love found later in life, typically in middle age, as the second time round after a divorce and a lot of accompanying water (consisting of tears, most like) has flowed under the bridge. And one crucial feature of it tends to be that the male party has snagged his adolescent carapace on the thorns of earlier experience, thus leaving it behind him, so that he can at last begin to match his psychological to his chronological age, enabling him to make a better job of doing what being properly in love requires – namely, knowing how to give and accept love well. Those are skills that only come with practice.

A Turkish proverb says that young love is from the earth, late love from heaven. This does not imply what the ancient Greeks would have thought it did. They welcomed maturity because, they said, it released them from what they regarded as the insanity of sexual passion. This is one of the relatively few things that the old philosophers got wrong. Not only does such passion remain, but the leavening of experience makes its expression a richer thing for everyone concerned.

No, the heaven of the Turkish saying is not the 'deep peace of the marriage bed' which is said to follow 'the hurly burly of the chaise longue',[30] but rather the clarity that arises from certain fundamental realisations about a relationship. In addition to recognising the other's individuality and need for space, there is also the appropriateness of sensible compromises, the value to be placed on kindness, consideration and generosity of spirit, the importance of making time to be properly in touch with each other, and in general the larger wisdom that accumulates with experience. Out of these ingredients much more profound attachments can grow, as durable as they are deep.

Even in later life there are of course no guarantees of maturity, least of all when it comes to the great ocean of human feelings with its submerged reefs. (Voltaire pointed to a bed and said, 'There is the rock on which the ship of marriage founders.') The singer with her refrain 'I've looked at life from both sides now' tells us she recalls only illusions, and still does not know life itself: that can happen. But plenty of people who have looked at both sides can report that the chances of loving and being loved more fulfillingly than ever before improve with experience.

Thus might the voice of experience speak. But in many relationships, early or late, the phenomenon that appears to have most disruptive and even destructive power is sex. Since the dawn of history societies have festooned sex with prohibitions, taboos, rules and restrictions. One of the major effects is to subordinate women, confine them, deny them the same scope for life as men, and thus deprive history of half its potential. The taboos and restrictions have magnified the importance and power of sex even further, and small amounts of it can, as a result, have massive consequences for marriages, political careers and churches.

The roots of the Judaeo-Christian moral tradition lie in the experience of the early Jewish people as herdsmen. Since the increase of the flocks was a matter of life and death, it mattered that male seed went nowhere but into females, with the possibility of thus impregnating them. The principle was extended to the government of human sexual relations. The serious wrong was misdirection of the male seed – to another male, or onto the ground as with Onan, whom the deity killed for this crime, because he was meant to be impregnating his dead brother's widow in order that children should be raised to his name.

In the Old Testament it did not matter if a man had sex with slaves or concubines as well as his wife or wives (Solomon had a large number of these latter), because pregnancy was always a possibility; but woe betide the man whose seed went in the direction of man, beast or nowhere. And woe betide the adultress or fornicatrix: she would be stoned to death.

One entailment of this view is that rape is not as bad as masturbation, because at least the former can result in pregnancy. Rape was a widespread phenomenon in the past, even more than in advanced countries today, although very often the female victim of it was held responsible, as in today's Pakistan and Afghanistan with their especially repugnant versions of Islam.

Sober reflection suggests that if sex were allowed a more natural place in human life it would take up far less time and make far less trouble than it currently does. Even in the more relaxed and mature societies of the world attitudes to sex and sexuality consume too much social oxygen, with the result that unnecessary harm is caused.

Nature has made sex pleasurable not just to ensure repro-duction but, in some of the higher mammals at least, to create bonds. The narrow views of the ancient Jews and the modern Catholics, that sex must always have pregnancy as a possible outcome, miss a very important point here. The closest rela-tives to humans are bonobo chimpanzees, which engage in sex almost as a greeting, casually and often. Unlike them and humans, sexual activity among other mammals is governed by the oestrus cycle, which makes females interested only when ready for pregnancy. As far as anyone can tell, other animals do not spend much time agonising over sex: they get on with it when nature and opportunity provide the prompt.

Human sex is more complicated, of course, because of the tangled social fabric surrounding it. Before effective contra-ception it was potentially a huge investment for a woman to have sex, and the biologists are keen to point out the addi-tional evolutionary reasons that make men naturally more promiscuous than women. Just how promiscuous men might be if given the chance is perhaps illustrated by certain kinds of male homosexual activity of the 'cottaging' variety, involv-ing frequent promiscuous encounters without much or any emotional attachment. The thought is that heterosexual men might behave as their homosexual brothers do if they did not face the restraints imposed by potential female partners.

It is now recognised that effective contraception and greater economic independence have together wrought significant changes in attitudes to sex among women. Moralists decry the increased sexual freedom that results, and point to accompanying increases in sexually transmitted diseases, and greater instability in partnerships and marriages, as the penalties being paid. But on the other hand it might be said that less frustrated and more experienced grown-ups

make better choices about long-term relationships eventually, and that anyway pleasure is a good – and sexual pleasure
a great good – providing it is responsibly done: and if responsibly done, it is hard to see the objection.

As this suggests, sex is not an ethically neutral activity. On
the contrary, it carries a high ethical value, which is that
when it is consensual and responsible, and governed by the
principle that those engaging in it must not do harm, it is a
deeply valuable thing. How can it not be, when it can so well
bring people together in intimacy and delight?

The downsides of sex have more to do with the psychological, legal and social interfering that is constantly in play
around it, one chief result of which is that the rationing and
constraining of it causes warped responses of various kinds,
including weird sexual behaviours, addiction to pornography, rape and sexual violence. It is absolutely typical of any
human interest that if it is thwarted it will bulge or leak or
mutate through the cracks in the constraints – drugs and sex
are prime examples of how prohibition and repression make
things vastly worse than they need be.

People are much more interested in sex than knowledgeable about it, which is part of the reason for the problems it
can cause. Ignorance about it is the result of prudery, prudery is the result of demonisation of it by religious moralists,
and alas they have the support of some philosophers too:
Aristotle claimed that sexual ecstasy subverts rationality, and
since rationality is mankind's highest and most distinctive
characteristic, it follows that sex is a threat to our very essence.
Lust and desire are the central paradigms of irrational urges
in human beings, on this view, and it was not long before
moralists generalised the threat to reason into a threat to
social order and therefore the authority of society's masters.

It is no surprise that laws and customs constraining sex and sexuality have been a preoccupation in most cultures.

There were economic considerations too, as there always are. Men of wealth wished to be sure that the children who inherited their riches were indeed children of their own bodies. So women had to be virgins when married, and kept inviolate afterwards. What men themselves did was not important, and typically they have always had far greater licence in sexual matters. But not as regards homosexuality: this was an especial obsession in the religions. In the early nineteenth century gay men were hanged in England for sodomy almost as readily as for murder;[31] in today's Iran homosexuals are hanged from cranes in public view.

Even heterosexual sex still kills. In Saudi Arabia and Afghanistan adulterers are still put to death, and by the cruel methods of beheading or stoning. These are the extremes; in most countries 'obscenity' is still an excuse for censorship and criminal proceedings.

Is it any surprise that sex is embrangled with hypocrisy, exploitation, anxiety and perversion, that tabloid prurience has a happy marriage with avid public curiosity, and that the progeny of this obscene marriage is the destruction of careers in politics and other fields if anything other than the most anodyne and conventional forms of sex is in the offing?

Taboos, prurience and restrictions persist despite the fact that so much is now understood about sex as a result of serious scientific research, and despite too the public education afforded by documentary programmes and the franker discussion of its place in life in literature and cinema.

Such developments provide useful perspectives, but they have not yet finished their work. In the United Kingdom public nudity is a crime; public exposure of genitals by a live human male is the most serious such crime; public portrayals or representations of an erect male penis are illegal. Everywhere in the world elaborate legal and social barriers control how, when and with whom sex is permissible. Sex is policed by society as if it were an explosive form of terrorism.

In the confused and sometimes unhealthy discussions that have frequently surrounded sex, two things have always prompted particular anxiety in moralists: homosexuality and prostitution. Both gays and sex workers have been a target for oppressive and reactionary attitudes, not to say punishments, in most places and for much of history. Because sex holds such a central place in moral concern, deviations from a supposed norm are regarded with special opprobrium, with the result that early in the history of social management of sex the moralists were able to turn not just social disgust but the force of law against both.

It is an oddity that our culture should be so vehemently anti-gay given our simultaneously held view of classical Greece, which we admire and claim as our cultural ancestor. The Greeks not merely permitted but encouraged homosexuality, and not merely homosexuality but pederasty, which in addition to its romantic and sexual aspects was intended as a form of male socialisation in which older men trained boys in the ways of the *polis* and the duties attendant on membership of it.

The latter is a custom many will think well superseded, and for good reason. But we allow other and even worse things to persist to this day: the genital mutilation of millions of boys and girls in religious practices of circumcision. The standard case against homosexuality is that it is 'unnatural' because (say its opponents) the way male and female sex organs are constructed and arranged 'shows' that sex should only take place between men and women. If something's being unnatural were enough to outlaw it, circumcision would be outlawed. In fact circumcision is vastly more unnatural than homosexuality, which is observed in quite a few species in nature. Likewise opponents of gay sexual life say that the male body is not 'for' receiving the sexual attentions of another male. If this 'for' argument carried weight, then since human legs are not 'for' riding bicycles, bicycles and the riding of them should be outlawed.

These points demonstrate that invocations of 'nature' provide no ground for opposing homosexuality. The real source of opposition is religious, and religious opposition succeeded in institutionalising social and legal sanctions.

Prostitution has had a more chequered history even than homosexuality in the evolution of societies. At times it has been welcomed, even admired; ancient societies had temple prostitutes, Venetian courtesans were greatly accomplished and celebrated as such, and the art and music of nineteenth-century France would not be the same without them.

In Anglophone countries we are still, here in the twenty-first century, in the legal bind introduced by the Victorians and their immediate successors regarding sex work and drugs. They prohibited drugs and placed severe restrictions on sex workers, and thereby gave an immediate gift to organised crime, in the process exacerbating most of the difficulties they thought they were expunging. All that such sanctions do is to massage the prejudices of moral conservatives.

It is hard to imagine how societies would get by without hypocrisy. Society has always implicitly recognised what is unappetisingly called the 'hygienic' function of prostitution, which is that it provides an outlet for people (mainly but not exclusively men) who do not have sexual partners otherwise, and it also satisfies the need for variety and sexual adventure in married men, thereby saving marriages. When divorce was impossible or difficult, prostitution not only saved marriages but also the institution of marriage.[32]

One would think that an important safety-valve like sexual services would be respected and even funded on the National Health Service. But it is the Anglo-Saxon way to manage these things in secret and shame. Any politician who suggested liberalising prostitution laws, especially by allowing women to work together in the safety, warmth and comfort of broth-els instead of being vulnerable and alone on the streets in the rain, would be crucified by the tabloid press. It would not matter a jot that the health and safety both of practitioners and of clients would be enhanced, or that it would end the wastage of police time and clogging of the legal system. No, there is a knee-jerk attitude to it which makes sensible reform impossible.

There is no doubt that some of the women who take to sex work are coerced, by pimps or by poverty or drug addic-tion, into doing what they find repugnant and wish they could escape. Such people urgently need help. Driving them underground is not a good way of providing that help. Some women enter sex work voluntarily. If they are raped or beaten and go to the police for redress they are as likely to be arrested for what they do as helped for what has happened to them. That is wrong, and yet another mark of the upside-down nature of the attitudes that most intelligent politicians know are wrong, but cannot change.

Pornography is defined as 'sexually explicit material designed to cause sexual arousal'. The same people who think that prostitution can be stopped by criminalising it or its practitioners and clients think that the same applies to pornography. They would do well to consider countries with liberal laws on pornography, asking themselves whether social implosion, epidemics of sexual violence and crime and the breakdown of human relationships have resulted. Indeed they might ask themselves the same about their own societies as a result of the ready availability of pornography on the internet, on which it is the largest single type of content.

Since the end of the world has not been brought about by pornography in either case, one of the main arguments against it collapses. There are two better arguments against it: that it purveys abusive images of women, and exploits the people involved in its production.

These are important points, but they are important because they are about abuse and exploitation, not because they are about sex. Abuse and exploitation are evils, whatever the abused and exploited people are doing or making – child labourers stitching footballs in Asia, or underpaid workers in an American factory.

Perhaps the clearest example of the harm caused by prohibitionism is drugs.

The criminalisation of drugs is a perfect example of how illiberal morality creates rather than solves problems. I mean the kinds of drugs which, like cocaine and heroin but unlike such equally dangerous drugs as alcohol and nicotine, are outlawed, making criminals of those who use them, and offering billions of dollars' worth of opportunity to organised crime while turning countries like Colombia and Mexico into murder zones, along with the streets of many Western cities.

It happens that neither the use nor the abuse of drugs, legal or otherwise, is a moral problem. It is a practical one. Quite differently, the *abuse* of drugs – including alcohol and nicotine – is an ethical problem. The target of contemporary debate and action about drugs is accordingly about ninety degrees wrong.

A drug is anything that alters states of mind or mood. This covers all three main kinds: narcotic, stimulant or hallucinogenic. Actually many substances have these effects, only in much milder form: caffeine is one example, sugar another; indeed you might say the same of any foodstuff.

The reason why some substances are controlled by law and others not has nothing to do with principles. The distinction is an accident of history, and is otherwise arbitrary. Alcohol and nicotine are as dangerous to health as the other substances, arguably more so in a number of cases. Some alcoholic beverages are said to have health benefits in small quantities – wine, for example – but so do marijuana, the opium derivatives and cocaine for analgesia. The reason that alcohol and nicotine are legal while other substances are not is simply that they have been used more widely and probably for longer in Western societies, and efforts to outlaw them have proved unacceptable to the public, and therefore a failure.

Drugs first came under legal control in England in 1868, not to outlaw them but to protect the professional status of pharmacists, who wanted the sole right to sell them. Opium was a widely used medication, mainly in the form of laudanum, and heroin was developed from it towards the end of the century. Soldiers in First World War trenches abated the horror of their circumstances by using opiates, or if they wished to bolster their courage or merely help themselves to stay awake they used cocaine, a substance also employed by Freud and Sherlock Holmes respectively in fact and fiction. The soldiers' activities prompted the passing of a Defence of the Realm Act to ban the sale of these drugs to the public. The 'war on drugs' thus began as a way of ensuring that men would be fully able to perpetrate the horrors of a real war.

For decades before 1914 moral campaigners in Britain and America had been working for the prohibition of alcohol, although in England there was also a society for the suppression of cocaine. The First World War was their chance. In the United States the monstrous folly of Prohibition followed – the outlawing of the sale and consumption of alcoholic beverages – and with it laws in most Western countries against opiates, cocaine and marijuana.

Since then many more substances have joined the list; others have been invented to replace them and then these were added to the list; and so on. When such laws were first enacted the incidence of drug use and abuse was fairly small, and addiction was regarded as a medical rather than a social problem. One major result of the prohibition approach has been rapid growth in drug use, through effective marketing by criminal organisations and the charm of the forbidden.

The United States' Prohibition disaster should have taught the world to think differently about this kind of strategy. Not only is prohibition an invitation to crime on a massive scale, but it makes criminals of millions of ordinary people too, with a staggering bill in policing costs and human lives.

Consider the contrast between the costs just mentioned, and the revenues that would come from taxing and regulating all drug use in exactly the way alcohol and nicotine are regulated and taxed. And then think of the difference a legal drugs industry would have on Colombia and Afghanistan.

Decriminalisation would solve the huge problems caused by prohibition. What would follow? Would entire populations suddenly become heroin addicts? Of course not.

Most of those who wish to take drugs already do it; most people who regularly take the kinds of drugs that are currently legal – alcohol, nicotine, caffeine – do it sensibly, and lead normal lives despite their addictions and consequent health problems. Regulation is preferable to prohibition: that is a lesson so firmly and conclusively taught by history that the fact that prohibitionist practices continue is unconscionable.

I suggested that drug *abuse* is an ethical, not a moral, problem. I mean by this that people who rely on drugs (of whatever kind, legal or otherwise) to attain well-being or to escape problems are in a poor case. Either they genuinely need the community's help, and should get it, or they lack what it takes – mainly, the intelligence or the courage – to attain life's satisfactions through the use of their own abilities.

I think it is a humanistic view to hold that people should not be too dependent on 'fixes' for their reliefs and satisfactions – the syringe of heroin, the glass after glass of whiskey, even the sleeping tablets and tranquillisers provided on prescription. Real reliefs and satisfactions come from relationships, the use of intelligence, curiosity and enquiry, activity directed at doing something or making something worthwhile. This, in fact, is a point about autonomy: someone whose life has been taken over by a drug addiction, whatever the drug, is at its mercy and under its enslavement. This is a *heteronymous* life – the opposite of an autonomous one – that is, a life governed by something external to the person living it. The good life must surely include self-government to the maximum degree consistent with membership of a surrounding community. A life of drug dependency is not only not such a life, but fails to be one in a very unappetising way.

There is another and quite different consideration in play here. It is that forbidding people to eat or drink what they wish, however silly or dangerous to themselves, or forbidding them to seek certain pleasures, however degraded, is a flagrant violation – a breathtaking one – of the privacy of the individual. Of course it is legitimate for a society to agree limits in certain respects, just as one does with alcohol: on the age at which people can make responsible choices about using such substances, and their responsibility for the consequences of doing so. The ever-present constraint is that what we choose to do must not harm others. There is plenty of justification for regulating matters in the way we regulate drinking, but none for forbidding them – even if they are, ethically speaking, contemptible ones.

Prohibition is the reverse of the coin whose obverse is prescription. They go together: the moralists tell us or try to tell us what we must and must not do, what is permitted and what is not allowed. Their refrain is '*I* believe such and such, therefore *you* must live accordingly' and '*I* do not like so and so, therefore *you* are not allowed to do it (or see it or smoke it or experience it).' Great frameworks of 'do this' and 'that is forbidden', of 'thou shalt' and 'thou shalt not', have been imposed on humanity in a variety of ways and forms, often cutting right across the grain of human nature, constraining and limiting it, and therefore causing the stresses that burst out into problems. It is like a chain reaction: because sexual relations were corralled by the church into monogamous marriage, the resulting problems associated with adultery, prostitution, marital breakdown, even incest and child abuse, either followed or were exacerbated. These were then punished in their turn, requiring more apparatus of moral and legal policing, shame, disgrace, jail terms, death sentences – the accumulation of wrongs because of the initial wrong is a lesson in the depths to which human stupidity can go.

A humanistic outlook says that the right attitude to the complexities that arise from human needs and desires is to insist on responsibility and the Harm Principle. We should recognise the imperatives at work in human relationships, and seek to accommodate them with the minimum of harm to third parties or indeed the involved parties themselves, and if – as will inevitably happen on many such occasions – there is hurt and the failure of pre-existing relationships, to manage these with sympathy and kindness, in the hope of redressing the balance sooner, and giving everyone involved a chance to reset themselves on the route to flourishing. What in practical terms this would involve is a case-by-case matter; but the principle is to accept that these things happen, to understand them, and to bring the best from them when time and opportunity offers.

19

Humanism, Death and the Ends of Life

There is as sharp a distinction between 'dying' and 'death' as there is between life and death. That is because these two distinctions are in fact the same one, for 'dying' is a living act, something we do while alive, even if at the very end of being alive. This makes an enormous difference both ethically and morally. Death – being dead; no longer being alive – is a fact that makes an *ethical* difference of great importance, which is that it gives life a definite and inevitable term, requiring of us that we do not waste our time in the project of seeking to live well.

Dying is a *morally* relevant matter of equally great importance, because in our age of sophisticated medical procedures and resources, no one (barring those who die in accidents or war) should have to die uncomfortably, suffocating or in pain, embarrassed or helpless. In short, euthanasia – which we should understand as 'a good dying' – should be available to all of us, and not least to the ill and old if they desire it (not if someone else desires it for them). The arguments in support of this view follow below.

People do not usually link questions about the end of life with questions about abortion, but there is a link, which is that both are about choosing to bring a life to an end because there are powerful reasons of an individual nature to do it – reasons, that is, that have to do with the meaning of an individual's life to himself or herself.

People who dislike the degree of autonomy this imputes to individuals to decide about the life or death of themselves or a foetus in the womb do not seem to have quite the same scruples when it comes to war or judicial execution. In war, when soldiers kill other soldiers (and hapless civilians who get in the way), and in judicial executions, the reasons for bringing a human life to an end might be considered problematic by some, but there is a strange general consensus of a shoulder-shrugging kind that these events should not be too closely inspected morally – these things just happen in war, such folk say; and similarly they seem to accept as inevitable and even reasonable that some countries have draconian ways of dealing with serious criminals (in most of those countries this category includes gays and adulterers), ways that they have accepted as lawful, and since it is their internal affair we cannot say much about it.

There is an interesting pair of alignments implicit here. Conservative moralists oppose euthanasia and abortion, but can consistently be in favour of, or at least untroubled by, the killing necessitated by war and capital punishment. Liberal moralists are for euthanasia and abortion, but tend to be against war and judicial execution. What explains these contrasting orientations?

The key has already been suggested. In the case of wishing an easeful death, and in the case of choosing not to have the immense unwanted consequences that flow from a pregnancy (note that: it is not the pregnancy but the difference made by it to the whole of the rest of a woman's life that is the unwanted thing), there is a thinking human individual whose judgement about his or her own life, and the impact on it of the major circumstances it faces, which is the essential matter. The discussion in earlier pages of the fact that it is up to individuals themselves to inject meaning into their lives, by their own choices and efforts, is centrally relevant here. Terminal illness (of which infirm old age is a subspecies) and pregnancy are two of the biggest things that can bend the trajectory of a life ninety degrees from the path that an individual has earlier mapped out. Sometimes people accept the change unexpectedly imposed on them; sometimes they choose to remain on track with the commitments and obligations marking that path, or – in the case of someone wishing to die while still in control of their own destiny – wishing to remain true to its character.

It would be extraordinary – I would say unthinkable – for someone else, let alone a stranger, to dictate to the individual in question that he or she cannot choose to intervene in that circumstance. But that is what religious moralists do in trying to end the right to abortion, and in standing in the way of legalising physician-assisted suicide. This is an egregious example of the '*I* don't like it therefore *you* are not allowed to do it' mentality which is what makes moralism of that kind so profoundly objectionable.

Accidents might bring mercifully swift and unrealised ends to life; one of the few good things about old age is that it might make the prospect of death attractive, or it might make the person in question forget that there is such a thing as death altogether.

But alas it can also be that the experience is sometimes a very difficult one, full of distress. The hospice movement is a wonderful thing, and the advance of medical knowledge has made pain manageable in most cases; but there are still aspects of dying that are wretched for the individual experiencing it, and scarcely endurable for those who love the dying person and witness the suffering involved.

Pain is not the only enemy of an easeful death. The feeling of not being able to breathe, being incontinent and in need of the ministrations of carers to be cleaned, feeling a terrifying helplessness, indignity and utter dependence that is only going to be relieved by death itself, being drugged and unable to relate properly to family and carers from beneath its muffling effect, all this can be profoundly upsetting to the sufferer, who might therefore wish for a neat, painless conclusion rather than being dragged on and on in the midst of the futile struggle that nature puts up against extinction.

There is an idyllic but not idealised contrast to this picture. A person knows she is going to die, and feels the onset of the symptoms that will very soon be difficult to bear. She is able to say goodbye to all those she cares about, and they to her. In one actual case I know of, the friends and family of the lady in question wrote her farewell letters communicating all they wished to say, and they visited her in her last week, and she and they were all able to address the question of her life and her death, and their relationship with both. Then she was able to compose herself, and when ready slipped calmly from life, her family holding her hands, and reading to her quietly as her breathing slowed and finally, imperceptibly, stopped.

This chosen and dignified exit is what is desired by people who go to Switzerland to have the assistance available there. It is frankly a disgrace that people cannot have the same simple amenity in their own homes in their own homeland if they have a clear and settled wish to avail themselves of it.

The case described is one of assisted suicide, which is the best form of euthanasia because it is consciously desired and chosen by the subject. Involuntary euthanasia occurs when someone is not in a position to express a wish either way, but is in a very bad state and is therefore either helped to or allowed to die. (In some British hospitals the legend 'No 222' on the record card at the end of a bed means – or at one time meant – 'no resuscitation'. The number 222 was the emergency number summoning the resuscitation team.)

There are many circumstances where involuntary euthanasia is justified, and it is quite commonly performed even in jurisdictions where it is illegal, for human pity is stronger than the law. Nevertheless many of the dying are condemned to suffering by the main anti-euthanasia argument, which is that legalised euthanasia *might* be abused.

Indeed it might. Human beings are frail and full of faults; the timber of humanity is crooked: anything and everything can be abused. But it is also within the wit of humankind to devise ways of managing matters to minimise the chances of abuse. As things currently stand, the tail of anxiety about abuse is wagging the dog of compassion towards those who wish to be helped out of their distressing and – in such cases – unendurable circumstances.

Euthanasia's opponents claim that inconvenient old people, tiresome to their relatives and filling up hospital beds needed by others, will be put down like unwanted kittens; that the sick or depressed will ask for death whereas if they lived, they might come to view matters differently and be glad they did not die; that a person might choose death just weeks before a medical discovery that could save him.

The result of these thoughts is prolonged suffering for thousands, perhaps for tens of thousands. These are terribly cruel scruples. Even less easy to forgive are the religious opponents who, in insisting that only a deity can give and take away life, are happy to accept that the deity is pleased to allow some people a hideous passage from this world to the next, when human kindness could so easily do a better and more moral job.

The euthanasia debate is a vexed one only in rich countries with the medical know-how that makes dying easy. There is little such discussion in poor countries, where death has to come, in any of its guises, pleasant or horrible, irrespective of what those who are dying would wish in the way of an exit. The problem of wealth and advanced resources is that it raises this acute dilemma: should we do what we can do? Does 'can' ever mean 'must', and if so, when? The obvious answer is 'No'. But in this particular case the question is, 'Why are we not doing what we can do, when what we can do can be so merciful?'

Humanism is for mercy, for respecting the autonomy and wishes of the individual, for recognising that dying is a part of life and therefore merits the full respect that life merits.

Dying and entry to the state of death is change, in itself no more or less. It is the return to nature of the elements that made the body, the chemical matter dispersing into the life of the world in all its variety of leaf and stream, air and light. To the individual who has died, death is the same dreamless sleep that existed before conception. Our deaths are nothing to us once they have come; while we live they are an important fact on the horizon that must give shape and determination to all that we do on the way towards them.

That is one of the two main meanings of death. Its other main meaning lies in its effect on the living who are left behind to grieve. For them the consolation is that a life is never lost to history; it happened; if the mourners will, after a time and not too long after, resolve to remember the best of the life that has been lost, and do what the person who had lived that life would wish for them – to continue living, to be happy, to succeed in their projects and desires – they will not allow the all too natural and inevitable presence of death in our world to keep them long from living as fully as they may, while they yet live.

If we base our view of death on evidence and reason, we see it as a natural process: the ceasing of bodily functions, including consciousness, followed by the body's dispersal into its physical elements, remaining part of nature but in a different way. Cessation of function and the beginning of physical transformation occur together at the moment of death; exactly what constitutes that moment is a controversial matter, an important one because sometimes medical practitioners need to know when to declare death, especially if there is a possibility of organ donation. The end of life has become ambiguous because many physiological functions can now be sustained artificially. But there is some agreement that brain death is the definitive boundary.

In the rest of nature the ceasing of function, followed by transformation of the physical elements, is not so much death as an essential component of life's continuity: death and decay are the servants of life. Fallen leaves fertilise the soil in which next year's seedlings grow: so the transformations of autumn are essential to spring. Death is therefore the basis of life and fully half of its rhythm.

To us the death of human individuals appears different from the death of other things, because whereas fallen leaves and blown petals constitute a cycle we can see as benign, the loss of a whole human narrative, the ending of relationships, the grief caused, the irrevocable nature of that ending of a chapter, has no parallel in nature. People are self-conscious beings, and regard death as a loss of supreme possessions: awareness and agency. It is not that most people, if they thought about it, would really wish to live for ever; Shaw's Methuselah suggests that endless existence would be intolerable. Rather, it is that death comes too soon for the great majority of us, before our interest in the world and in those we care about is exhausted.

Because being dead is indistinguishable – from a subjective perspective – from being unborn or from dreamless sleep, it can hold no terrors. What seems frightening is the act of dying. But dying is a living act, and as with any other such it might be pleasant or unpleasant. That is why the existence of ways to make dying easy – means of euthanasia – should be available to us all if we desire them. But being dead is no part of our personal experience. Death is what happens to other people. We experience *dying* for ourselves; but we experience *death* only in losing others, and the experience is one of grief and loss. Accordingly, our own deaths are no part of our personal experience: each of us experiences only life, of which dying is part. In this sense, from the subjective perspective we are immortal.

Marcus Aurelius, Roman emperor and Stoic philosopher, said in his *Meditations* that to die is only to lose the present moment, for the past has ceased to be and the future has not yet come; so to comfort ourselves we have only to ask, 'Is this moment really worth keeping?' But I do not think

Aurelius is right. At each moment we are each of us a meeting point of memories, plans, prospects and hopes, so the present is a large and important place where past and future are focused together, and we are defined by the relationship of our pasts to our current efforts, and of these to our expectations. We are creatures of narrative; the next instalment of the story is of crucial interest to us, which is why we mainly regard death as an evil, whether of someone we love, or as the limit of our own lives and endeavours.

To those who wish for death and welcome its advent, by contrast, the present moment's mixture of all the past and a bleak future has its shape distorted by anguish. Suffering of any kind, but in particular of the terminal and unrelievable kind, invites our compassion: what we can give to the present of such a sufferer is relief, release, the kindness of a helping hand.

Most religions teach belief in an afterlife. Familiarly, what their votaries are taught to believe is that their posthumous existence begins with a judgement that results in punishment or reward, and for the vast majority it will be punishment, for sin lurks in every crease and fold of the moments of physical existence. Such ideas are very useful for controlling the living. Some find these ideas psychologically supportive; others find that they make death a more terrible prospect: death becomes a dangerous country, ruled by strange powers, into which we creep nervous and ill-prepared. It sometimes happens that the more devout or credulous a believer is, the more horror the inevitability of death holds for him: I have personally known people tormented by their sense of sin and their terror at what will greet them when they die. It is an unspeakable cruelty.[33]

Plato took the view that citizens should be encouraged to believe in a blissful afterlife for heroes so that they would make good soldiers.[34] There are several forms of religious enthusiasm that share this view. Islam is a case in point; it promises that death in *jihad* grants direct entry to paradise, with various further enticing rewards thrown in (of a kind forbidden on earth, incidentally, which makes this aspect of Islamic morality a puzzle). In these cases also, therefore, religious superstitions about death prove useful to priests and kings.

Because, on a naturalistic view, being dead is identical to being unborn, nothing about death in itself makes it good or evil. It is what it takes away from us that makes it one or the other. If it takes away suffering, it is good; when it takes away hopes, possibilities, relationships with those beloved, it is bad.

Some argue that one's own death is never bad, because, being dead, one is unaware of what is lost. It is the prospect of that loss which makes death a bad thing, not the fact of it; so death once again is a problem only for the living. It is an avoidable problem, therefore, for one can take Spinoza's point that 'the meditation of the wise man is a meditation on life, not on death'. He means, rightly, that one can avoid fear of dying by accepting its inevitability and then putting thoughts of it aside in order to concentrate on living. Among other things this avoids the coward's fate of dying in imagination a thousand times over.

The fundamental question for us all is how to deal with the deaths of others. When we grieve for someone who was important to us, we are grieving the loss of an important part of what made life meaningful to us. Recovering from grief takes a long time, a time that has to be endured. It is marked in many societies by formal periods of mourning, between one and three years long. But the world is never again entire after grief. We do not get over losses; we merely learn to live with them.

But there are consolations. The coupled facts that the dead once lived, and that we loved them, are written indelibly into the record in their connectedness. They are facts that can never be effaced from time. If one wished for eternity, that is the best kind one could imagine.

Ordinary observation of nature's cycles must have been a source of hope for early mankind, faced with the enigma and unpleasantness of death. Resurrection stories are common-places of religion and myth. They – so to speak – kill two birds with one stone: they give personal hope of surviving bodily death, and they give hope of being reunited with lost loved ones. As noted, this can be counterbalanced by dread of judgement and punishment too. The latter makes the release and ultimate rest of oblivion a far more welcome alternative. It is a far more welcome alternative also to the saccharine horrors of what convention attributes to heavenly bliss.

Votaries of religion shake their heads sadly at comments like the last. How little those atheists imagine, they say, what it would be like to spend eternity with one's god – what 'bliss' might mean, and what suffering to be deprived of it! But the truth is that they do not know what they mean by this either, but though it is vague in content their belief in it is all conviction.

In truth, few of the living are much good at dealing with death, especially in this contemporary age with its pretence that death does not happen and that happiness consists in purchasing power. Few think of it clearly, still less face it squarely. Because most people just assume that death is an invariable evil, they refuse to allow that those who suffer should be allowed its merciful embrace if they choose it, seriously and soberly.

Those unfamiliar with the latest developments in Christian theology will be surprised by some of the things now meant by 'eternity' and 'conquering death' in the rhetoric of the contemporary church. For example, some theologians now interpret biblical references to 'eternal life' to mean 'living in eternity', that is, turning one's back on the distractions of the world and living a life of religious devotion, realising eternity in the here and now and thus making it a style of living rather than a future state. 'Conquering death' is accordingly redefined: it no longer means surviving bodily death and passing spiritually into an afterlife; it means ceasing to fear death by ignoring it (in effect, Spinoza's advice: the advice of an atheist).

No discussion of death can fail at least to glance at what appears to be evidence for the existence of an afterlife, so-called 'near death experiences'. Reports of these are increasing in number because medical advances mean that more people who have been seriously ill or injured can now be revived from cardiac failure than ever before. Despite the similarity sometimes apparent in stories told by people who have been medically resuscitated (of passing through a tunnel towards a light, encountering helpful beings and perhaps deceased relatives – though the stories tend to be culturally conditioned: Christians meet Jesus but Jews and Hindus do not; they meet other figures or none), the evidence is anecdotal and – most importantly – does not relate to death but to an extremely stressful episode in life. For that reason careful assessment is needed of the effects of drugs, physical and psychological trauma, and disturbance of brain activity, in understanding the nature and aetiology of the hallucinations (if that is what they are) that these factors provoke in combination; but the starting point has to be that they are indeed hallucinations, before they are ruled out and more exotic explanations are sought.

Depending on how one counts them, something between 800 and 3,000 new religious sects, or even new *religions* as such, have sprung up since the Second World War, most of them in the United States and Africa. A frequent feature is that they are not much concerned with an afterlife, because they are millenarian, believing that the end of the world is imminent, and they promise anyone who will join the sect that he or she will be transformed, raptured or otherwise saved when the end comes. But when they do teach the existence of a heaven, these new religions tend to describe it in terms (to quote one author) of 'golf-courses, stress-eradicating pastimes and such leisure pursuits as may be had by means of wealth in the best areas of California'.[35] What the author could have added is that features not very different, though adjusted for period, characterised Christianity's heaven in the early days of that faith.

What explains belief in life after death? Too often, either or both of these powerful motives: fear, and a yearning for justice. The first is self-explanatory. The second seems less compelling for people who live in relatively safe and comfortable rich countries. Their residents forget that, for the vast majority of people, today as throughout history, existence is a labour, and sometimes a grim one. The civilised voices that echo down to us from the past are those of the literate few who had opportunities to speak or act, which they did at the expense of great masses of faceless, nameless strugglers with little to hope but that, in another and different dimension of existence, they might have a chance of happiness and relief. In short, the existence of hopes for and belief in an afterlife constitutes a very sad reflection on the harsh facts for the majority of mankind in this life.

It is the latter fact above all others that makes a humanist think that the focus of our collective energies should be on making this life more like the heaven that exists in the imagination of those who are weary and heavy-laden; for that is how best to refresh them.

The apparent belief that it is length – which means: quantity – of life that matters prevents us from asserting the priority of quality of life – more accurately: the quality of experience – over mere quantity. That is why the idea of allowing people to choose a good dying if they wish it is so important. We have to accept that in physician-assisted suicide, as in all things human, there can be mistakes and abuses. But one act of genuine mercy, in which we help someone escape agony, indignity or any form of acute suffering, justifies itself by the mere fact of being merciful.

I suggested that although 'euthanasia' literally means 'a good death' it would be better to define it as 'a good dying'. Either way, everyone hopes for euthanasia in the end, usually by preference a naturally occurring death, an easy and painless passing from life after a healthy old age. But when dying is difficult, a struggle, horrible to experience, euthanasia has to come by other means.

'Euthanasia' is standardly understood to denote only deliberate acts which result in someone's death, but it also means the withholding of acts that would prevent death, as when an elderly patient with pneumonia is not given antibiotics, or when a life-support machine is switched off, allowing someone in a long-term persistent vegetative state to die. This is called 'passive euthanasia' and is regarded as lawful and acceptable. Active euthanasia takes place when someone is given death-inducing treatment of some kind, and is not regarded as lawful and acceptable in most jurisdictions.

But there is, in fact, no moral difference between the two kinds of euthanasia, because deliberately not doing something is as much an act as doing something. The concept in theological ethics of 'sins of commission and omission' embodies a recognition that equal responsibility attaches to deliberate withholdings of action and choices not to act, just as it does to failing to act when action is required. In that important respect passive and active euthanasia are no different. They both involve deliberate choices, and they both have the same outcome.

It is merely a matter of sentiment that passive euthanasia is regarded as more acceptable, and it is a sentiment of lay-persons and moralists rather than those engaged in the care of the suffering and dying. These latter know how often active euthanasia is actually carried out. The failure to shorten the sufferings of a patient in painful or frightening terminal phases of an illness is so cruel that few medical practitioners refrain from doing something to help, at very least in increasing levels of analgesics or sedatives to the point where vital functions are suppressed. Not to do this would be to treat people with less consideration than we treat animals; we regard it as humane – humane! – to end the lives of animals swiftly and easily when their suffering is unrelievable otherwise. It is a happy fact for human sufferers, every day in hospitals all over the world, that doses of medication are raised to fatal levels when needed, the legitimacy of the exercise protected by the 'doctrine of double effect' which says that because a medical practitioner's primary duty is to alleviate suffering, the life-shortening side effect is inescapable and therefore acceptable.

But as with the distinction between passive and active euthanasia, the doctrine of double-effect is a mere conceptual fig leaf. Stating that one's intention is to relieve pain rather than shorten life in such cases is a sleight of hand, given the empirical certainty that the act will cause death. Why not accept that hastening the advent of death is the ultimate form of pain relief, if no other chance of recovery exists; and is therefore a legitimate part of the treatment to relieve suffering?

In discussion of physician-assisted death, whether direct in the sense of passive and active euthanasia, or brought about by 'double-effect', the point is frequently made that medical practitioners are bound by their professional ethics to save, protect and promote life, or at least to minimise the suffering incident on accident or disease – and not to kill. There is a clause in the Hippocratic Oath – still invoked in the United States and implicit in medical practice everywhere – that states, 'To please no one will I prescribe a deadly drug, or give advice which may cause my patient's death.' The principal significance of this is that the practitioner binds himself or herself not to give in to pressure, whether from family or political or other kinds of interests, to end the life of someone who does not wish to die. But some readings of the Oath have it say that a practitioner will not accede to a patient's own request to die either, and this is the reading invoked by opponents of physician-assisted suicide. Yet it seems obvious that a practitioner who refused to help a patient to die who was in otherwise unrelievable suffering, and had a clear and settled wish to be helped from his predicament, would be failing the Hippocratic duty to aid the patient. This suggests that the appropriate reading of the Oath is the third-party one.

This said, it remains that there is a genuine and honourable concern among many medical practitioners about engaging in euthanasia, given that their chief and overriding duty is to save life, to ameliorate suffering, and to cure ills and injuries, if they can. A practical innovation might therefore be suggested: that there should be a medical sub-division of anaesthesiology which night be called 'thanatology' (to coin a word from *thanatos*, death), and that these specialists should work within a framework of law under the supervision of hospital ethics committees, so that every thanatological treatment is approved in advance, monitored during administration and properly recorded afterwards. Since only thanatologists will be involved in helping those who have shown a stable and intelligent desire to be helped to die, all other medical practitioners will continue to work under the assumption that their sole concern is to save life, cure ills and palliate suffering. This will clarify the grey area in which many medical practitioners currently work, given the frequency with which, for compassionate reasons, they administer life-shortening treatments.

At the other end of life, in connection with the question of abortion, matters are complicated by our instinctive tenderness towards babies. 'Pro-life' campaigners make frank use of emotional appeals in describing abortion as baby-murder. The truth is that abortion is almost always a very difficult choice, for it does indeed involve the deliberate termination of a form of human life. But this does not make it invariably wrong. There are many hard things we have to do that are

justified or – more strongly still – necessary; and this can be
in the name of compassion too, for the claim of a foetus
always competes with the established responsibilities, interests and goals of a human individual.

There are clear-cut justifications for termination of pregnancy in the case of genetically compromised foetuses or
endangered mothers. A pregnant schoolgirl offers a more
difficult case, but surely the rule here should be to prefer the
actual commitments and projects of a present person – the
girl herself – over the multiplying cells within her which at
very most represent a potentiality.

That does not make the potentiality of no interest; we
accord rights even to the not-yet-conceived when we say
that future generations have a claim on us to protect the
environment in their interests. It follows all the more strongly
that the conceived have claims too. This means that abortion
can never be taken lightly. But few people take abortion
lightly. For those faced with the dilemma it is a matter of
choice between continuing their lives as then situated, or
undergoing the dramatic and whole-life change that parent-
hood involves – even when the child is given away for adoption, because the psychological burden of that can be greater
than the other choice.

Opposition to abortion is not exclusively religious, but
religious motivations are one of its chief sources. Life is
regarded as god-given, and therefore 'sacred', and therefore
its deliberate ending is taken to be a serious sin. This view
appears not to allow that to create a lifetime of suffering is a
far greater sin, as it is – say – to force a woman already over-
burdened with other children to add to their number. For
the humanist it is not the 'sanctity of life' (rarely invoked by
those who oppose abortion when talking of capital

punishment and war) but the *quality of life* that matters; and this last figures centrally among the justifications for abortion, because it applies to the life already being lived by the person carrying the cells within.

This last thought gives us a way of working through the dilemma that abortion poses, by considering how we are to adjudicate the conflict of interests involved.

On the one hand there are the serious occurrent interests of an existing adult or near-adult individual woman, who has plans, commitments, needs and obligations which bear on the question of whether she is in a position to continue her unwanted or inopportune pregnancy, and to raise the resulting child or give it away for adoption. Either way she is faced with a life-changing intervention in her current circumstances.

On the other hand there is a developing foetus, at that stage a set of potentialities, and no more, as a future human individual. Of course both mother and foetus have rights to the protection and consideration of their interests, but the key is whether those rights are equal. Reflection on the contrast just drawn strongly makes it clear that the mother's interests so far outweigh those of the foetus that her right to have them protected must prevail when they compete.

There is, to repeat, nothing happy about the situation people find themselves in when an unwanted pregnancy occurs. Nature is highly profligate with foetuses, spontaneously aborting the majority of them in the early phases of pregnancy; and yet in other cases, more rarely, it is miserly with them, denying them to women who long for a baby but cannot conceive. It is hard for these latter to look with equanimity on the tens of thousands of abortions voluntarily performed every year. But the kindest among them would recognise the possibility of lifelong tragedies for pairs of people, and usually for more than the pairs involved, that could exist if there were not resources for terminating unwanted pregnancies in a world of many difficulties and burdens.

20

Religion Revisited

Because so much of the moralistic outlook in preceding sections has its root in religious tradition, a further comment on it is appropriate. It was earlier acknowledged that there are no doubt sincere believers who find solace and inspiration in their faith, and who do good because of it. They must find it painful to reflect on the spectacle of religion's terrible record of bloodshed, cruelty and intolerance − throughout history, and still in this present day. But because religious belief does not rest on rationality but on emotions − hope, fear, feelings of absolute certainty or agonising doubt, psychological needs of various and importunate kinds − it is unsurprising that faith visits violence on what it regards as heretics and other enemies.

We saw also that for most votaries of religion, the roots of their faith lie also in a distant past of ignorance, superstition and accompanying myth-making. These brought into being taboos and rituals, concepts of obedience and disobedience to the tenets of the faith: and this is what gives religion-influenced moral thinking its content.

But religion is a bad source of moral insight. This is not least because it is in fact either irrelevant to questions of morality, or it is positively immoral. This claim undoubtedly seems contradictory or merely polemical at first, but reflection shows otherwise.

Consider the primitive form of Christian morality as set down in the New Testament, which collects the religion's foundational documents. In a few respects it is the same as all other moral systems, in enjoining brotherly love and charity: that is a commonplace of any reflection on what would make for good lives and societies. But then it differs, with its own particular set of injunctions: give away all your possessions, take no thought for tomorrow (consider the lilies of the field), do not resist anyone or anything evil (turn the other cheek), obey the authorities (render unto Caesar), turn your back on your family if they disagree with you, do not marry unless you cannot contain yourself sexually. This is the morality of people who genuinely believed that next week or next month the world was to end, that this world does not matter – indeed, is ripe for the furnace – and that one should ignore its demands and realities.

This is not a liveable morality. The additions of the church, claiming to have continuing authority in revealing the deity's requirements, add further irrelevances and distractions. To live as a serious person in a world of many difficulties and demands, one needs something vastly richer and deeper than these anchoritic nostrums. Hence the irrelevance claim.

The immorality claim comes hard on its heels. When fundamentalists of one or another religious tradition deny rights to gays, deny education and health care to women, practise genital mutilation, amputate limbs as a punishment, stone adulterers to death, use murder against those they oppose, extol suicide bombing and acts of terrorism in the name of their faiths, religion becomes positively immoral.

Much religious energy is devoted to interfering in and controlling sexual behaviour, either by prohibiting most forms of it, together with representations and even thoughts of it, or by preventing sensible management of its consequences, as in the case of abortion. In countries where the religious cannot stone or imprison those they regard as sexual malefactors, they send the press complaining letters about nudity on the cinema screen and teenagers buying the morning-after pill, while ignoring the fact that automatic rifles, handguns, shells, cluster bombs and rocket launchers are being exported from the country they live in to regions of the world gripped by poverty and civil war. With such examples and contrasts, religion has little to offer moral debate.

The fallacy in thinking that a deity is required to provide grounds for morality was noted earlier. The point can be reprised in Bertrand Russell's succinct remark, 'Theologians have always taught that God's decrees are good, and that this is not a mere tautology: it follows that goodness is logically independent of God's decrees.' It might be added that if the will of a god is the ground of morality, one's reason for being moral is merely prudential; it consists in a desire to earn the reward of heavenly bliss, or to escape punishment. This might be sensible if there were a powerful and punitive agency watching whether we obey its wishes, but it is not a satisfactory basis for ethical life; threats and promises are never logically compelling premises for any argument.

Consider the major religion familiar to most of us in Western countries: Christianity. It is an oriental religion whose irruption into the classical world eventually overwhelmed it and changed its course dramatically. It is interesting to speculate how the history of the West might have proceeded if Christianity had expired, after a short time, as

merely another version of various common and ancient
Middle Eastern myths, in which a god makes a mortal woman
pregnant who then gives birth to a hero who attains heaven
after mighty or miraculous deeds – recall Zeus's many mortal
paramours and their offspring – and including the dying and
reviving god theme, as in Egypt or the myth of Persephone;
and so endlessly on.

For one thing, if Christianity had gone the way of other
mythologies of its time, Plato's and Aristotle's academies in
Athens would not have been closed down in 529 CE because
of their 'pagan' teachings. The irony attaching to this occurrence is that their suppresser, Justinian, was the builder of the
Church of the Holy Wisdom in Constantinople.

For another thing, there would have been no Christians to
put a stop to the Olympic games in 393 CE because of their
dislike of athletes' nudity.

Apologists might say that without the accident of
Christianity becoming the Roman Empire's official religion,
we would be without the glories of Renaissance art. But
balance against this the blood-soaked character of much
Christian history – its crusades, inquisitions, religious wars,
drowned witches, centuries of oppression – and this comes
to seem a debatable matter. In place of Annunciations and
Madonnas, Crucifixions and Resurrections, we would have
more Apollos Pursuing Daphnes, more Deaths of Procris,
more Dianas Bathing. By almost any standards, apart from
the macabre and gloomy ones of Catholic kitsch, an Aphrodite
emerging from the Paphian foam is an infinitely more life-
enhancing image than a Deposition from the Cross.

The religious attitude is an odd mixture of literalism and
selective blindness. It says that certain writings are holy, either
the word of god or written under divine inspiration, but

then it refuses to take seriously what the writings say. Read this passage from the Book of Samuel – in the King James version, a beautiful piece of prose – and ask whether, if what it reports exemplifies holiness, it encourages us to behave likewise: 'Then said Samuel, "Bring ye hither to me Agag, King of the Amalekites." And Agag came to him delicately. And Agag said, "Surely the bitterness of death is passed." And Samuel said, "As thy sword hath made women childless, so shall thy mother be childless among women." And Samuel hewed Agag in pieces before the Lord in Gilgal.'

If the mincing of Agag caused divine pleasure, then surely Goethe's Prometheus is right: 'I know nothing more wretched under the sun than you, ye gods! Scantily you feed your majesty on sacrifices and the breath of prayer; and you would starve if beggars and children were not hopeful fools.'

Leslie Stephen observed that while religion flourishes, the only ethical enquiry there can be is casuistry, the enterprise of interpreting divine commands. The ultimate justification of these commands, promising rewards if obeyed and threatening punishments if disobeyed, therefore rests on a logical fallacy, the *argumentum ad baculum* or threat of force. But, as repeatedly noted, promises and threats are not a logical justification for acting one way rather than another.

Religious apologists claim that our motive for acting morally should not be the threat of divine punishment, but love of god and our fellow men; we behave well as a response to the fact that god loves us. However well-meaning this way of putting things, it is camouflage. For if someone chooses not to act on the prompting of such sentiments, or fails to feel them at all, he is not therefore excused punishment. He will suffer the fate of the fig tree which was cursed for bearing no fruit out of season.

For the humanist it matters to ask this: if interest in and concern for one's fellows is a reason for being moral, what relevance does the existence of a deity have? Why cannot we accept that we are prompted to the ethical life by these natural human feelings? The existence of a god adds nothing, other than as an invisible policeman who sees what we do always and everywhere, even when alone in the dark, and who rewards and punishes accordingly. Such an addition to ethical thought is hardly an enrichment, since among the under-pinnings to the moral life they offer are threats – of fear, of exclusion, even of violent sufferings: which are, among other things, exactly what the moral life seeks to liberate us from. These threats characterise the state of mankind under religion for most of history; liberation from them, and therefore from religion, is a desideratum of humanist morality.

Religious styles of morality were premised on a religious view of the universe and mankind's place in it. Before the seventeenth century's scientific revolution people found that egocentric view of the universe a satisfying one. They believed that it had been created by a deity expressly for human beings, who were, beneath heaven anyway, the summit of that creation. When it was proposed by Copernicus, and empirically demonstrated by Galileo with his telescope, that the Earth is one modest member of a vast swarm of astronomical bodies, occupying an insignificant corner of a huge universe, the affront to human self-importance, and with it therefore to the primacy of theology, was incalcula-ble. But the calm deductions and patient observations of science, together with its fruits in practical respects, did not make opposition to it plausible for long.

A non-religious ethics – a humanist ethics – is very differ-ent because it places humanity in its natural setting, with all that this implies for thinking about the good. It means that there is an obligation on us to understand our own nature and circumstances; that is the force of the point that the considered life, the informed, reflected upon, and chosen life, is best.

If it were argued that religions set moral examples unparalleled by secular ideologies such as political movements, the claim would be easy to reject; religions fare worse than some secular outlooks, and much worse than others – much worse than humanism, for example, which has killed no one for disagreeing with it. There have been no wars fought over differences of opinion in botany, and historians do not stockpile nuclear weapons for use against one another, other than figuratively.

One is tempted to quote 'by their fruits ye shall know them'. One of the chief threats posed by religious militants is the allegation of blasphemy, to the extent even of justifying murder – think of the contemporary origins of this scandal in the Salman Rushdie affair. It is now, alas, a commonplace of our world again, most especially when offence is taken or sensitivities inflamed, especially on the part of Muslims.

The word 'blasphemy' derives from two Greek words: *blaptein* and *pheme*, the first meaning 'to injure' and the second meaning 'reputation'. It has been used to refer to libel or defamation against ordinary people and institutions, but over time its primary meaning has come to be 'any word of malediction, reproach or contumely pronounced against God'.[36] This is an interesting definition, given that reproaches against the gods must live daily in the mouths of suffering mankind.

It always takes two – an utterer of a viewpoint, and someone to take offence at it – to make blasphemy possible. It is

the product of conflicts between perceptions. The perceptions are subjective, born of tradition and located at the heart
of cultural identity.

Because what counts as blasphemy depends on relativities
and the non-rational subjective commitments of faith, it is
not a fit matter for law. Blasphemy laws, like those relating to
obscenity and censorship, are instruments for controlling
ideas and the expression of them. They are invariably harsh;
Pakistan's laws decree the death penalty for 'defiling the holy
Qur'an' and making 'derogatory remarks about the Prophet'.
Compare this to now-repealed nineteenth-century laws in
certain states of the United States, where the penalty for
anyone who 'wilfully blasphemes the holy name of God by
denying, cursing or contumeliously reproaching God, His
creation, government or final judging of the world, or by
cursing or contumeliously reproaching Jesus Christ or the
Holy Ghost, or by cursing or contumeliously reproaching or
exposing to contempt and ridicule, the holy word of God
contained in the holy scriptures' was anything up to a year in
jail and a fine not exceeding $300.[37]

Technically speaking, Christian punishment for blasphemy
should be the same as in Pakistan. Leviticus 24: 16 says that
the blasphemer is to be put to death, and Luke 12: 10 says
that blaspheming against the Holy Spirit is unforgivable, a
claim supported by Mark 3: 29 where it is deemed an 'eternal sin'.

Laws against blasphemy violate the most fundamental of
civil liberties, namely, freedom of expression. Without freedom of expression all other civil liberties are empty. There
cannot be democracy without free exchange of information
and vigorous debate involving criticism and challenge. There
cannot be due process at law unless people can speak freely

in claiming their rights or defending themselves. There cannot be proper education unless people can enquire, discuss and criticise freely. Art and literature would be sterile. In short, without freedom of expression only a monochrome and stagnant society would be possible, as is the case everywhere tyranny reigns over people's minds and tongues.

It is not an accident that what made the modern world possible was the progressively great freeing of minds and tongues in the sixteenth and seventeenth centuries CE in Europe, in often deadly danger from the church and its partner the absolutist state for heresy, blasphemy and treason.

When dispassionately considered, those aspects of religious ethics which are peculiar to their religious character and not shared with other moral systems, including non-religious ones, cannot be said to add up to much. As noted above, the morality of the New Testament is thin and in practical terms unlivable. Nietzsche argued that the Beatitudes, which assert that the poor, the meek and the downtrodden are especially blessed and will receive their reward in heaven, manifests the psychology of an enslaved people – he meant the Jewish nation as it was in Egypt before Moses – and he might have added that it has well served the rich and powerful throughout history, since it reconciled the poor and humble to their lot, and helped to prevent uprisings.

What Christianity offers in the way of a positive moral outlook is very similar to the Judaism that preceded it, and the Mohism of ancient China with its ethic of brotherly love and its concern for widows, orphans and social justice. But neither Judaeo-Christian nor Mohist ethics compares to the richness and insight of 'pagan' Greek ethics, or to present-day concerns about human rights and animal rights, which are much broader, more inclusive and more sensitive than anything envisaged in religious morality.

This last point is especially significant. Religious ethics is based on the putative wishes – more accurately: commands – of a supernatural being. For the humanist, the source of moral imperatives lies in human sympathy. If I see two men do good, one because he takes himself to be commanded to it by a supernatural agency and the other solely because he cares about his fellow man, I honour the latter infinitely more.

21

Humanism and the Ethical Dimension

The question of how one should live and what sort of person one should be is an ethical question, not a moral one. It is a question of how to live flourishingly as a whole person, and in ways that respect the choices of others and their differences from oneself. The fullest consideration of this question has to take into account the moral negotiation that ethical individuals enter into; and that naturally and rapidly evolves into questions about the kind of society they should jointly constitute, to ensure that ethical lives can flourish within it.

These were themes that both Plato and Aristotle, in their very different ways, focused on. For the empirically minded and pragmatic Aristotle, the task was one of examining the institutional structures that would allow individuals the chance to live lives of practical wisdom in accordance with reason, the differentiating essence of humankind. For Plato, by sharp contrast, the ideal society would be one organised into castes of statesmen ('philosopher kings'), warriors, tradesmen and labourers, in which each individual had a single function consonant with his ability, assigned in childhood, for which eugenics were practised, so that couples were chosen for the task of procreation and their offspring would be raised in state nurseries; and the only drama and poetry allowed would be such as extolled virtue and the example of good and courageous heroes.[38]

Plato's profoundly unattractive version of a rigid and authoritarian society is one that would not have allowed his own teacher, Socrates, to exist; that is the irony of it. Socrates was a questioner, a challenger, opposed to the authority of conventional ideas. In this respect he belongs to the tradition of 'Pre-Socratic' philosophers, despite the label which separates him from them, because the distinguishing mark of the Pre-Socratics was their rejection of the habit of deferring to past authority – the traditions and legends that provided an account of the origin, nature and purposes of the world – and their intention to free the mind of man from mythical thinking. The Pre-Socratics asked and answered questions about the world which were radically confident; they took it that observation and reason could together provide ways of understanding the world far better than myths of gods and giants.[39]

Socrates is separated from the Pre-Socratics not because of any difference of intellectual attitude, but because of a great difference in intellectual interest. Whereas his forerunners were concerned to theorise about the nature of reality, Socrates was concerned to discover how one should live. Their concern was metaphysics, his was ethics. It took many centuries before developments in method and technique allowed metaphysics to become physics and its companion sciences, but the ethical concern was fully fledged in Socrates. For the thousand years of Christian domination of the mind of Europe there was little ethical thinking – religion had all the answers, and enforced them, not encouraging question or challenge, or efforts to think about foundational matters unless they conformed to (indeed, deferred to) the authority of the faith – but when minds began again to be free in the birth of the modern world from the sixteenth century onwards, there was a return to these essential questions, and the Socratic mood was able to revive.

That mood is the humanist one: to question, to consider, to take responsibility for choices, to work things out in the conversation of society about how the good is to be realised.

This happens against the background of hard facts. Whereas the majority story of human community is a positive one – counting together the experience of life in almost every village, town and city in the world, every day, there are millions of acts of kindness, courtesy and mutual co-opera-tion, even among strangers – the minority story remains: the story of man's inhumanity to man. It is a tragic common-place of human history. In the twentieth century there was an amplification of its effects because technologies had become available for it to be expressed on scales and in a manner hitherto scarcely imaginable. The difference was one of degree, not of kind; if egregious figures like Genghis Khan and Tshaka the Zulu had had machine guns, mustard gas, bomber aircraft, Zyklon B, nuclear weapons, or any of the other technologies of modern mass murder, they would certainly have used them. Theodor Adorno is said to have remarked that the development of these technologies show that humanity has grown cleverer over time, but not wiser; in his remark the example is that the spear has developed into the guided missile, an ominous transformation that sharply illustrates his point.[40]

But it is only one of the tragedies of our times that

technological development has outrun moral development. The other is that the liberties won for individuals by the Enlightenment project of the last three centuries are too often abused by too many into licence; not least in the economic sphere.

Even the darkest clouds, though, have their silver linings. The experience of the twentieth century's two world wars, and especially the crimes committed by Nazism in the years between 1933 and 1945, prompted real urgency in thinking about how to apply concepts of rights in practice. Legal (as opposed to 'merely' moral) conceptions of 'crimes against humanity' and 'genocide' had to be fashioned practically from scratch for the Nuremberg trials; together with debate during the war years about a Universal Declaration of Human Rights, these ideas and their application were marks of progress even in the depths of chaos and slaughter.

Critics who think that modern times are wickeder than earlier times typically blame the change on a loss of moral tone, which in turn they blame on the waning of religious commitment.[41] Some regret the lessening of religion's influence not because they themselves have a faith outlook, but because they think that the existence of a religious presence in community affairs fosters a better moral climate. This belief is widespread, and weighs with those, whether secular or not in other respects, who think that faith-based schools will improve the discipline and self-restraint of children.

Because of what was said above about the relation of religion to morality, there should be no need to explain again how traditional religious moralities are in fact not to the point, for morality has to be grounded and justified independently of claims about the existence of gods or other supernatural agencies and what they are said to demand of their creatures. Rather, moral ideas have their life in the relationships between human beings in social settings. It is in the conversation, negotiation and mutuality of social life that moral norms and practices actually emerge; and when in addition to moral debate each individual has a mature concern for the ethical – the personal choices and aims that take responsibility to others deeply into account – circumstances exist in which a good society has the best chance of emerging.

That last remark implies the central fact: that the ethical underwrites all else in morality and society. In turn, the central question of ethics can be variously put as: what sort of person should I be? How should I live? What is my route towards, and contribution to, the good?

Philosophy is one significant place where the conversation about these questions can fruitfully take place, because it is the inheritor of the tradition of this debate. Literature and the arts make an even greater contribution; what is learned in the social sciences and, increasingly, in some areas of the natural sciences, is indispensable.

There was however a serious failure by moral philosophers, especially in the analytic tradition of mainly Anglophone philosophy, who reacted to the twentieth century's horrors of war and atrocity by claiming that it was not their job to continue Socrates' debate about the good and how people should live, but rather (so they said) to examine the concepts and terminology of moral discourse, together with the logical relations between moral propositions.

Those philosophers were partly right: there is a need for careful analysis of moral concepts and of the kind of reasoning

– practical reasoning – used in working out what *should* and *should not* be done – these being terms of obligation. And some brilliant insights have been offered in the course of scholarly debate about these questions. Some of those who refused to adopt the role of teacher or guru did so for the admirable reason that, once the terms of moral discourse had been clarified, it was up to us all to think for ourselves on the basis of this improved understanding of them.

That too was right. What was wrong, however, was the break in continuity with the tradition of applied thinking about the good life which Socrates initiated and which was developed by his successors from Aristotle and the Stoics to the Enlightenment.

Fortunately, the continuity was not entirely lost; for even as some university philosophers were turning attention away from the practical questions which, by their very nature, is what ethics and morality are about, outside the university was growing up a variety of discussions under the collective label of 'applied philosophy', foremost among them medical ethics, business ethics, environmental ethics and debates about animal rights.

These discussions are prompted by the need to think about how to live and choose in a world beset by the problem of change happening so fast and in such complex ways that it overtakes our ability to comprehend and manage it. Many if not most of the problems we face in economic activity, in medical practice, in war and conflict, are the result of being *able* to do things that we are not entirely sure we *should* be doing; but because the fact that we can do it so often unthinkingly forces a 'yes' answer to the doubtful question, 'shall we do it?', we find ourselves in moral turmoil, chasing our principles after the practice has already begun.

But it is never too late to think, and to try again, and to reverse course if necessary: it requires the assertion of intelligence and good will, the resolve to continue the progress – if need be, the struggle – towards the good. This too is a tenet of humanism.

22

The Better Alternative

The fact is persistently overlooked that those who are not religious have available to them a rich ethical outlook, all the richer indeed for being the result of reflection as opposed to conditioning or tradition. Its roots lie in rational consideration of what humankind's cumulative experience teaches; and that is a great harvest of insight.

The foregoing pages have argued that humanism is premised on humanity's best efforts to understand its own nature and circumstances. The outcome of those efforts shapes what humanists aspire to be as ethical agents. They wish to respect their fellow human beings, to like them, to honour their strivings and to sympathise with their feelings. They wish to begin every encounter, every relationship, with this attitude, for they keep in mind Emerson's remark that we must give others what we give a painting: namely, the advantage of a good light. Most of our fellow human beings merit this, and respond likewise. Some of course forfeit it by what they wilfully do. But in all cases the humanists' approach rests on the idea that what shapes people is the complex of facts about the interaction between human nature's biological underpinnings and each individual's social and historical circumstances. Understanding these things – through the arts and literature, through history and philosophy, through the magnificent endeavour of science, through attentive personal experience and reflection, through close relationships, through the conversation of mankind which all this adds up to – is the great essential for humanists in their quest to live good and achieving lives, to do good to others in the process, and to join with their fellows in building just and decent societies where all can have an opportunity to flourish.

And this is for the sake of this life, in this world, where we suffer and find joy, where we can help one another, and where we need one another's help: the help of the living human hand and heart. A great deal of that help has to be targeted at the other side of what the human heart is – the unkind, angry, hostile, selfish, cruel side; the superstitious, tendentious, intellectually captive, ignorant side – to defeat or mitigate it, to ameliorate the consequences of its promptings, to teach it to be different; and never with lies and bribes.

Humanists distinguish between individuals and the wide variety of belief systems people variously adhere to. Some belief systems (those involving astrology, feng shui, crystal healing, animism, religion . . . the list is long) they combat robustly because the premises of them are falsehoods – many, indeed, are inanities – and, even more, because too often belief in some of those falsehoods serves as a prompt to discord and strife, and at last even murder. Humanists contest them as they would contest any falsehood, any corrosive enemy to human progress and well-being.

But with the exception of the individuals who promote these systems when they should know better, humanism is

not against the majority who subscribe to them, for it recognises that they were brought up in them as children, or turn
to them out of need, or adhere to them hopefully (and some,
too often, unthinkingly). These are fellow human beings,
and humanists profoundly wish them well; which means too
that they wish them to be free, to think for themselves, to see
the world through clear eyes. If only, says the humanist, they
would have a better knowledge of history! If only they would
see what their own leaders think of the simple version of the
faiths they adhere to, substituting such sophistry in its place!
For whereas the ordinary believer has somewhat misty and
incomplete notions of the religion they subscribe to, their
theologians deploy such a labyrinthine, sophisticated and
complex approach, that some go so far as to claim that a god
does not have to exist to be the focus of a faith.

In contrast to the certainties of faith, a humanist has a
humbler conception of the nature and current extent of
knowledge. All the enquiries that human intelligence
conducts with the aim of enlarging knowledge always make
progress at the cost of generating new questions. Having the
intellectual courage to live with open-endedness and uncertainty, trusting to reason and experiment to gain us incre-
ments of understanding, having the integrity to base one's
views on rigorous and testable foundations, and being
committed to changing one's mind when shown to be
wrong, are the marks of honest minds.

In the past, people were eager to clutch at legends and
superstitions in order to attain a quick, simple closure regarding what they did not know or understand, to make it seem
to themselves that they did know and understand. Humanism
recognises this historical use of mythologies, and sympathises
with the needs that drive people to treat them as truths. It

points out that what feeds their hearts and minds – love, beauty, music, sunshine on the sea, the sound of rain on leaves, the company of friends, the satisfaction that comes from successful effort – is more than the imaginary can ever give them, and that they should learn to redescribe these things – the real things of this world – as what gives life the poetry of its significance.

For humanism premises the value of things human, without the assistance of illusions about anything supposedly beyond this world and its realities. Humanism's desire to learn from the past, its exhortation to courage in the present, and its espousal of hope for the future, are about real things, real people, real human need and possibility, and the fate of the fragile world we share. It is about human life; it requires no belief in an afterlife. It is about this world; it requires no belief in another world. It requires no commands from divinities, no promises of reward or threats of punishment, no myths and rituals, either to make sense of things or to serve as a prompt to the ethical life. It requires only clear eyes, reason and kindness; and with them a determination to make the world the best place it can be for the flourishing of creativity, good possibilities and the affections of the human heart.

Notes

2 Naming and Describing a 'god'

1 Exchange with Keith Ward in *Prospect* magazine, 20 February 2005.

4 An Axe to the Root

2 http://news.bbc.co.uk/1/hi/uk/699929.stm.
3 Frederick Douglass, 'The Significance of Emancipation in the West Indies', speech, Canandaigua, New York, 3 August 1857.

5 Knowledge, Belief and Rationality

4 This is the tack taken by P. F. Strawson in *Introduction to Logical Theory*, London: Methuen & Co, 1952 (Chapter 9 part II *passim*).

6 Agnosticism, Atheism and Proof

5 Bertrand Russell, *Look* magazine interview, 1953.
6 http://www.users.qwest.net/~jcosta3/article_dragon.htm.
7 W. K. Clifford, 'The Ethics of Belief', *Contemporary Review*, 1877.

7 Theistic Arguments

8 'Atheist' has for most of history been a term of such malediction, as a result of religious hostility, that it is only recently that atheists have begun openly celebrating their self-ascription of the title.

9 Arguing by Definition

9 Alvin Plantinga, *The Nature of Necessity*, Oxford: Clarendon Press, 1974.
10 Plantinga, *Where the Conflict Really Lies: Science Religion and Naturalism*, Oxford: Oxford University Press, 1974.
11 *New York Times*, 13 December 2011.

10 Causes, Wagers and Morals

12 Plato, *Laws*; Aristotle, *Physics* and *Metaphysics*; Leibniz, *Monadology*, 1714. For Plato and Aristotle see texts in the Internet Classics Archive; for Leibuitz, see G. W. Leibnitz, *Monadology*, trans. and ed. N. Rescher, London: Routledge 1992.
13 Pascal, *Pensées,*1670. See online Project Gutenberg edition.
14 Voltaire, *Remarks on Pascal's Pensées*, 1728. Nabu Press, 2012, trans. and ed. T. Smollett.
15 William James, *The Will to Believe*, 1896, criticised as giving 'an unrestricted licence for wishful thinking'.
16 Leibniz, *Discourse on Metaphsyics*, 1686. Hackett, 1991, trans. and ed. D. Garber and R. Arlew.

11 Creationism and 'Intelligent Design'

17 Andrew J. Petto and Laurie R. Godfrey (eds), *Scientists Confront Intelligent Design and Creationism*, New York: W. W. Norton, 2007.
18 This process began in the middle years of the first decade of the twenty-first century. See the report by Stephanie Simon in the *Wall Street Journal*, 2 May 2008.
19 Neither side seems troubled by the vagueness of 'proceed'. The consequences rumble on to this day, for one of many examples in the tensions between Serbs and Croats, who sit on either side of the immense disconnection caused by this little connective.
20 Stephanie Simon, *Wall Street Journal*, 2 May 2008.

14 Humanism and the Good Life

21 My *The Good Book* is intended to be a resource of just this kind.
22 This is a view shared by one of the twentieth century's finest philosophical minds, Bernard Williams.
23 Jean-Paul Sartre took such a view.
24 There were times in the story when, in the swing of politics, this was less so; Socrates was put to death when the Thirty Tyrants were in power, because he angered them. This could not have happened in Pericles' Athens.

25 While living in the Far East I was struck by the ethical importance attached to objects of vertu, ornamental gardens, ponds, vistas, calligraphy, poetry, flowers, insects, the pleasure of hearing rain on bamboo leaves or on the moss on a stone lantern, light playing on lacquerware. In all cases the point is the mindfulness involved, an alertness to the good to be found everywhere that one seeks it.

15 Putting the World to Rights

26 The Universal Declaration is a statement of broad principles. It was supplemented in succeeding decades by two Covenants, on political and civil rights and on social and economic rights respectively. These and several other instruments and agreements relating to rights together constitute an International Bill of Human Rights.
27 Disclosure: I am a member of this organisation.

16 Shared Humanity, Human Diversity

28 The *locus classicus* for these points is Alasdair MacIntyre, *After Virtue*, London: Duckworth, 1981.

17 The Ethical and the Moral

29 This is John Stuart Mill's 'Harm Principle', which for all its apparent simplicity is probably the single most important moral principle. In invoking it I should say the great sin is harm to other sentient creatures; but here I will restrict attention to human beings.

18 A Humanist on Love, Sex and Drugs

30 An insightful remark attributed to Mrs Patrick Campbell.
31 See C. Davies, *The Strange Death of Moral Britain*, New Jersey: Transaction, 2006 and G. Ross, *Strangers: Homosexual Love in the Nineteenth Century*, London: W. W. Norton & Company, 2004.
32 On this read Richard Posner, *Sex and Reason*, Harvard: Harvard University Press, rev. ed., 1995.

19 Humanism, Death and the Ends of Life

33 Walter Kaufmann pertinently says, 'It is interesting to ask more than two thousand years later to what extent the widespread terror of death is the aftermath of almost twenty centuries of Christianity.' Walter Kaufmann, *Tragedy and Philosophy*, Anchor Books, 1969, p. 16.
34 Plato, *Republic*, p. 386. Penguin, trans. Jowett.
35 Dan Cohn-Sherbok and Christopher Lewin, *Beyond Death*, London and Basingstoke: Palgrave Macmillan, 1995.

20 Religion Revisited

36 The Catholic Dictionary (De Relig., tract. iii, lib. I, cap. iv, n. 1).
37 This example is provided by Massachusetts.

21 Humanism and the Ethical Dimension

38 Plato, *Republic* and see also *Laws*. For Aristotle's views see the *Nichomachean Ethics* and the *Politics*.
39 See Edward Hussey, *The Pre-Socratic Philosophers*, Hackett, 1995, and the Diels–Kranz fragments.
40 More accurately, this remark is *attributed* to Theodor Adorno, though it is hard to find a source for it. He was hostile to the Enlightenment and humanism which he blamed for the ills of twentieth-century totalitarianism. In this he was mistaken, wholly so. See ch. 15 above.
41 They are wrong. As shown by Steven Pinker in his book *The Better Angels of Our Nature* (Penguin, 2011) there is overwhelming empirical evidence that the world has become a less violent and less cruel place as human history has unfolded. This development, despite the apparent contradiction of the twentieth century, has accelerated since the eighteenth-century Enlightenment, alongside the spread of secularism and the decline of religion.

Index

A NOTE ON THE TYPE

The text of this book is set in Bembo. This type was first used in 1495 by the Venetian printer Aldus Manutius for Cardinal Bembo's *De Aetna*, and was cut for Manutius by Francesco Griffo. It was one of the types used by Claude Garamond (1480–1561) as a model for his Romain de L'Université, and so it was the forerunner of what became standard European type for the following two centuries. Its modern form follows the original types and was designed for Monotype in 1929.